Life Reboot

AN INNER WISDOM GUIDE TO FINDING YOUR PASSION AND PURPOSE

ISBN: 978-0-9952573-0-6

Cover design and layout: Abria Mattina.
Author Photo: Brandon Elliot.

To every person who is seeking something more
out of life.

Acknowledgements

Thank you God, for without the breath of life, none of my experiences or this book would have been possible. Thank you to my family and friends for offering your love and support throughout my life and on this journey of writing my first book. Thank you Yogrishi Vishvketu for your laughter and for teaching me how to shine my inner light through yoga. Thank you Annika, as you have helped me to find my voice and to reshape this book into what it has become. Thank you Megan and Abria for your editing and design expertise. Thank you Barb, not only for your editing skills, but also for your friendship and for inspiring me to become a coach. Thank you to all of the wonderful people I have met on my travels, as you have been a part of my healing journey. Thank you to everyone who I have crossed paths in life with so far; you are all my teachers and I have learned something valuable from each one of you.

Contents

Chapter One Introduction

- October 7, 2008 – The start of the journey

Some people think I'm crazy for leaving behind a comfortable life and career for unknown territory, but here I am - I'm finally on my way! It's 3 a.m. local time in Dubai. There are lots of people in the airport, considering it's the middle of the night. I'm sitting on the floor counting the number of sleeping feet lined up next to me. I would join them, if only I had a blanket and more than one hour to spare before boarding my next flight to Delhi. This all feels surreal - it hasn't fully sunk in yet.

It's quite freeing to be traveling without much stuff. I have a backpack to my name and a couple of boxes that are being shipped from Canada to Scotland, where I'll start my new life after this trip. I'm off to India - a place I've never been to before. To think this all began because of a conversation with someone whom I've never met!

I have no idea what the future holds, but I'm excited to see what unfolds. More about this later as I just heard my flight announcement. Bye for now…

Heading into unknown territory

This was my journal entry as I embarked upon my first trip to India. My friends and family were mostly supportive, but not everyone was at the time. Maybe I was going through an early mid-life crisis at thirty-three years of age. I was feeling restless and didn't really know why. Looking back I realize now that deep down I wasn't feeling completely happy then, despite all appearances of a good life. Little did I know how much my decision to go there would change my life. I was going to India to learn more about yoga and to become certified as a teacher so that I could embark upon a new career when I returned. I was excited to travel more long-term as I had quit my job to explore a new country and culture.

I have always loved traveling yet had only managed to vacation for a couple of weeks at a time; six weeks was a luxury. I didn't realize the extent of my life changes until now. The further away I went from home and the longer I traveled, the more I journeyed within. The more people I met from different cultures, the more I learned about myself and about what I was really seeking: a deeper connection to myself.

Fast-forward nine years later, to 2017, today. I have finished transcribing all of my journals, which were the basis for me to write this book. Going even further back through my journals, even before that journey to India in 2008, I discovered I had intended to write a book a long time ago:

– June 14, 2002 – Planting the first seed

If I'm ever to write a book I suppose I will have to organize my thoughts into some sort of a story so people can actually understand the ramblings of my mind!

I wasn't really surprised when I came across the above journal entry written almost fifteen years before. Rather it was a silent acknowledgement, a deep sense of knowing that my 'someday' had arrived. I had casually entertained the idea over the years that 'someday' I would write a book, yet it seemed to be a far-off goal, something I might do when I retired, maybe when I reached my sixties. Now is all I have. I couldn't wait another twenty years to reach my sixties to do the things I love.

Challenging the status quo

If you're anything like me, you have probably questioned almost everything about yourself, about life and society's rules like expectations that you finish high school, go to university then work to save for your annual vacation, retiring when you're sixty-five. I wasn't even sure what I wanted to do in university. I started out in Business because it seemed to be the right thing to do. I then switched to Economics because I got kicked out of the Business Honours program in my second year for lack of effort and poor grades. I smartened up in third year, got my grades up and fast-tracked my way out of university into a full-time job.

I have always loved traveling, so two weeks of vacation per year didn't seem like long enough for me to explore the many places I wanted to visit. I was probably born a traveler. I love the excitement of getting on a plane or setting off on a road trip where I get to explore unknown territory and to meet new people. I often travel without a specific plan because this puts me out of my comfort zone. There is something exhilarating about arriving in a new place, not knowing anyone or speaking the language and having to rely on the kindness of strangers and my own resources to find my way.

The early years

I sometimes jokingly pin my love of travel on my parents as they had me traveling halfway across the world at the formative age of eleven, when we left our home in Ireland to start a new life in Canada. My parents grew up in the time of 'The Troubles' in Belfast. The Troubles, or the Northern Ireland conflict, began in the late 1960s and ended with the Good Friday Agreement in 1998. It was a guerrilla war between the paramilitary forces of the

Irish Nationalists and British Loyalists that was mostly political in nature with a religious dimension. The historical origins were much older than that.

The problem over the division of land started in the 1600s when settlers from Scotland and England were sent to the North of Ireland to farm on land that was confiscated from the Gaelic chiefs. It's mind boggling that so much suffering has ensued over the years during many wars in such a small region; a region with a population of about the same size as Toronto and slightly higher than Philadelphia.

While the conflict was mostly political over whether Northern Ireland should remain in the UK or unite with the South, there were tensions in some neighbourhoods between the Protestants and Catholics. Thankfully we were raised in a mixed neighbourhood and it didn't matter to me as a kid which church my friends went to. Ultimately my parents wanted a better future for us.

My grandmother often tells me the story of what I wrote on that day in my calendar on the 15th of May, 1986, with a sad face "leaving - this is the worst day of my life!" I was due to go to middle school and was faced with leaving my whole world behind, including my best friend Louise. I was convinced that I would never make any new friends in Canada and that life, as I knew it, was over. This was a significant time of transition for me; one where I later learned that life was not over and that I could roll with the changes as I settled into my new class in the small town of Camlachie, in south-western Ontario. I am grateful that my parents had the courage the change their lives for us, starting over in a new country with three young children.

Looking back over significant events in my younger life has made me realize that even though they might have seemed traumatic at the time, the events have provided me with strength and courage. They have moulded me into the unique person I am today.

What makes you unique?

Just like me, you have experienced events that provided you with your strength and courage. You have your own unique stories, experiences and perspectives on life that will differ from mine. There will also be similarities in our stories. I hope you will be able to identify with my story, to see something of yourself in it, and be inspired to look at new possibilities in your own life. This is not to say you must quit your day job and go travel the world like me. Instead I invite you to start reflecting on your own life and where you are at today. Leaving my job to travel the world is the path I chose to get to know myself, to listen to the yearnings of my soul and to follow my bliss, no matter how many people doubted me or told me I shouldn't do it.

Like me, you might be feeling restless with where you are, looking outside yourself for answers, or you may have been feeling that something's missing. I was often bored with my job and after a year or two with a particular company I was ready to move on. I was feeling deep down that there was more to life than what I was living. I was craving adventure and more excitement that I wasn't getting during my weekends off. While I had great friends and a full social life, I often had a sense of dread going back to work on Mondays. Many people think this is normal and accept this, however I didn't and I thought that becoming a yoga teacher and doing something that I loved would change all of that. As I had been practicing yoga for ten years at this point, I believed that if I got paid to do what I loved then it wouldn't feel like work and it would bring me a sense of satisfaction and pride.

Feeling frustration, stress, and loneliness

In the summer of 2008, I was feeling tired, stressed out and irritable a lot of the time. I was working too much and had reached the level of management in my tech career that I'd set out to achieve when I first started after finishing university. Being a manager came with increased responsibility and more business travel, which took me away from my friends and family for long periods of time. While I was mentally challenged at my job and I worked with some really talented people, being away from my close circle and living out of a hotel for weeks at a time in a small town was lonely. I missed cooking for my friends and having dinner parties; eating out at restaurants is a luxury and not something I enjoy doing every day. At least I was staying in shape as I had taken up running to pass the time during the weeknights. It was that or watch TV in my hotel room. What I didn't realize was that I was also dealing with addiction.

Dancing with addiction

Looking back, my life could have been very different if I had accepted the status quo. It was late in 2006 when I decided to leave the west coast of Canada. Not only did I choose to leave my job and social life, I also chose to break off my relationship with my long-term boyfriend; let's call him Adam. We met a few years prior at work and we instantly hit it off. He was warm and funny and incredibly social – always the life of the party. He quickly became a part of my life and it was less than a year after meeting that we were living together. Leaving him was a difficult decision at the time and I wondered if I had made the right choice. Looking back, my travels and subsequent experiences of healing let me know that I did.

The relationship started out well, as most do during the "honeymoon" period, however, over time the darker sides of our personalities began to reflect one another—and clash hard. There was a third entity in our relationship – a presence of ghosts from a past that he was trying to hide from by using cocaine and alcohol. Adam's own story is not mine to tell.

I liked my booze too but I felt like I was living a double life. On one hand I projected a good image during the day – I had a great job, lived in a beautiful apartment by the beach, lived a healthy lifestyle and had a good circle of friends. On the other hand I had a dirty little secret. I was coping with his addiction while developing one of my own by drinking and smoking pot almost every night, which countered all of the healthy habits I had during the day. I'm not blaming him for my addiction because I know now the root of it was because I was lacking a deep connection and feeling of unconditional love for myself. I was looking to fill the void with drugs, alcohol and even through my relationship with Adam.

We didn't have the communication skills at the time to get past the anger and fighting in order to learn from our mistakes and to heal together. Over the years I turned into someone I didn't even recognize – I was tired of being angry all the time. I wanted to love and support him, to make him change, but I couldn't and the control freak in me couldn't stand this. I became exhausted with worry over the times when he would disappear for days and I wouldn't hear from him. I became tired of the apologies and the promises of changing. I became tired of the emotional abuse. I eventually realized that I was enabling him financially and emotionally by staying in the relationship. There was nothing that I could to do force him to face his demons and to get help. Who would want to be forced to change by another person anyway?

The signs that this was not a healthy relationship were there all along, however I chose not to acknowledge them. Hindsight is great, isn't it?

In the year and a half since I left the west coast and Adam, I hadn't really enjoyed a relationship with a significant other; I had pretty much kept to myself. I went on the occasional date but nothing really stuck. I wasn't in a place of truly connecting with a partner. I believed at the time that I just hadn't met the right person. Now I know that I wasn't in a place to truly give myself to another person then. I still had much healing to do, even though I thought I was over my relationship with Adam. After all, I had left him behind when I left the west coast.

Reflection:

Take a moment to pause and think about what's going on in your life right now. What are you tolerating or putting up with in your life?

Looking back it's easy to see now that I was tolerating less than I deserved, yet I didn't consciously take the time then to examine my life to see what needed to change. I just wanted to get away and if I couldn't change my physical environment I was escaping it in my mind with alcohol and drugs.

Finding freedom in sitting still

The one thing that kept me grounded throughout all of this was my yoga practice. Since university, I had been attending yoga and meditation classes about once a week. I discovered that incorporating meditation into my busy life, by sitting quietly for a few minutes a day, left me feeling really relaxed and free. At the time I was finishing up university and I was working a part-time job. I had an active social life and I always looked forward to my weekly yoga class.

I wanted to explore yoga further, to experience more of the relaxing feeling that came after Svasana – the final relaxation pose. During a phone conversation with a family friend one night I decided right then and there I was going to the source – to Rishikesh, India to pursue a yoga teacher-training course. Rishikesh is considered to be the birthplace of yoga and is where the ancient Rishis (seers) began to explore their connection to themselves and the world around them over five thousand years ago.

The Rishis are sages or 'seers of thought', who had incredible powers and discovered through various yoga and meditation practices that there are many expressions of Oneness or Divine Consciousness. It's said they had a complete understanding of everything in this world and the after-world. Some of the foundations of Hinduism can be found in the teachings of anonymous ancient sages, which were primarily transmitted orally and have been documented in the Vedas; a collection of hymns and other ritual texts composed during different periods and dating back to 5500 BCE.

The phone call with our family friend when I made the decision to go to India was a pivotal point in my life because I went from going to yoga a few times a week to making yoga part of my daily life. During my first year of travels, through yoga I learned to harness the power of my thoughts to create better circumstances and opportunities in my life. Over time and with practice, I have also learned to love myself. Learning to love all parts of myself has been one of my greatest challenges. It's an ongoing journey as I continue to discover new parts of myself to accept and love.

As you embark upon your own journey with me through this book, you will learn more about yourself. At times this could be uncomfortable, or it could be liberating. My hope is that you learn to love and accept yourself as you are, to embrace all of the wonderful quirks that make you unique. Through my journey I discovered parts of myself that I would have judged others harshly for, and I was most harsh on myself.

Yoga is a journey and a path to self-discovery, one that is still unfolding to this day. I no longer feel dependent on pot to feel good and I can enjoy a glass of wine without feeling compelled to drink the whole bottle. My daily meditation practice keeps me aware of my thoughts and I've learned that I don't need to give in to impulses. Meditation has also helped me to release old stories (samskaras) about myself that are no longer true. There's much more to come on samskaras in Chapter 7.

My inner and outer journey

You'll learn more about my inner journey, through meditation, and the outer journey of my travels, throughout this book. I circled the globe four times over the course of three years while teaching yoga. I landed some amazing jobs that were practically stress free. With a group of yoga teachers, we formed a charity – Helping Hands for India - under the direction of my teacher, Yogrishi Vishvketu, and we've built a school in northern India that provides free, quality education to almost three hundred children. All of this happened because I challenged the status quo, I challenged my thoughts and started saying 'yes' to opportunities that felt right, while going with the flow of life, instead of against it.

My inner wisdom has always existed yet I was either unaware of it or often ignored it before. When I undertook my first trip to India I began to learn more about the power of this wisdom within as I had plenty of time to reflect on my life. Wisdom comes to me in moments of quiet or stillness in the form of an idea, which could be an image or a single word. It also comes in the form of feelings and emotions that resonate in different parts of my body when I'm paying attention to what is happening now.

Tuning into my thoughts and understanding the wisdom of my body has helped me to lighten up, to pay more attention to the positive and to enjoy the abundance of life so much more—this allows me to live a passionate and purposeful life. This doesn't mean that I no longer feel stress or anger; rather, I've learned how to work with my emotions and to not let things fester. I've learned to take responsibility for my feelings and actions and to make changes when things aren't working, instead of looking to blame others or my circumstances. Most importantly, I've learned that I am the creator of my reality and my experiences. While I can't control everything that happens in my life, I know that I have full control over how I react to situations and how I engage with people, providing me with the power to create an amazing life with no limits.

Writing this book has been a journey in itself for me and my intent is to share my story and lessons with you, perhaps saving you years of frustration so you can start living a more passionate and purposeful life today.

> **Reflection:**
> *Take a few moments to imagine that there are no limits and everything is possible. There are no obstacles of time or money and you have no obligations. What would you be doing with your life? What's the wildest or craziest thing you can picture yourself doing?*

Your journey begins

You don't have to be a yogi in order to benefit from the information offered here and you don't have to have a burning life purpose either - some people know at an early age what they are meant to do with their time on earth, and others have many different purposes - it's about the journey, experiencing the now and helping you to get to know yourself. I want this to encourage you to be curious and to ask questions.

While reading this book you will have a chance to go on your own journey. When moving through the chapters, go at a pace that feels right for you. Some chapters may cause you to reflect for longer periods of time than others. You will get more clarity on your dreams and desires, and you will learn about common roadblocks that are holding you back from moving forward in your life. Finally you will be guided towards taking action so that your dreams are no longer fantasies in your head, but will become your reality, when you set your mind to it.

You will need a journal and pen to take notes, as there are exercises provided throughout which are designed to help you to reflect and to tune into your own inner wisdom for guidance along the way. Some exercises may take a few minutes and others could take longer, requiring deeper introspection. Your journal entries don't have to be perfect.

For the exercises presented in this book, we will be using the techniques of brainstorming and freewriting. Brainstorming is a popular technique used in groups to spark creativity by writing out ideas in the form of spontaneous lists – you can brainstorm by yourself as well. Writers and others, commonly use freewriting - where you write for a continuous amount of time (anywhere from 2-10 minutes) without any regard for spelling and grammar - to help overcome blocks of self-criticism or perfection. If you get to a point where you feel you have nothing to write, then write about the fact you have nothing to write – just keep the pen moving. I've solved many problems this way by writing a question in my journal then freewriting. When I'm not looking for the solution, it often comes out in my writing.

Let's start now

You can make a shift by using the power of your mind to send your life in a new direction today. How big are your dreams? What will it cost you not to pursue them? I want you to fast forward to your last day on earth and imagine looking back over what you are most proud of. Have you achieved this yet? Knowing that everything is possible and you get to define what is normal, it's time to unleash your personal power to bring your gifts to life.

It may not be a straight path forward for you; it wasn't for me. I experienced many ups and downs in my inner and outer journeys. I had to get real and to be brutally honest with myself when exploring the inner world of my thoughts, my habits, my perspectives and opinions of myself and of my life. It was necessary to go into the dark places in order to let my light shine. Let's go on this journey together so you can start living your life of passion.

Get out your
notebook!

Exercise: Dear Me

You will write a letter to your younger self. You may write whatever you wish and the letter can be as long as you choose. Use the following as a guideline and feel free to elaborate.

1. Write down today's date and your current age.
2. Dear (insert your name),
3. Note the age of your younger self or a period in your life that you are addressing.
4. What do you want to say to your younger self? Write down the first thing that comes to mind.
5. What wisdom would you like to share with your younger self? Perhaps choose one or two topics, rather than writing about everything you have learned since then.
6. Sign it with love. Keep the letter in a safe place. You may wish to read your letter again when you have finished this book, or at some point in the future when you are feeling reflective. Notice how you feel when you are reading the wisdom you have shared with your younger self.

Congratulations! You've completed your first journaling exercise.

Chapter Two

June 15, 2002 – Drowning in negativity

Why is it that some people accumulate so much stuff, yet others have nothing? What good is having money if you can't spread it around to help other people who so desperately need it? Why is the wealth of the world so unevenly distributed? Why do people kill each other for money, land, or power? Where does that get you at the end of the day?

It's another day of random thoughts and erratic writing – so fast that my pen can't keep up with what my mind wants to unleash. When I talk to people about these things, sometimes the response is a nonchalant "that's just the way the world is," or even worse, "that's human nature." I'm pretty sure I'm not the only person who gets pissed off hearing these answers – are we really all that selfish and uncaring? Bullshit!

Human nature is what we create - we create our own nature. We're rational beings, we have a choice in how we behave and we have a choice in how we react to situations. I can understand being angry with someone but being angry to the point where you lose the ability to communicate with and resort to violence, is not understandable.

There is no justification for taking another human being's life. What other species does this? What other species captures and tortures their own or makes them subservient just because they have a different point of view? Is it all about power and greed? I hear this every day in the news – no wonder it's difficult to maintain a positive attitude. I refuse to believe that people are predominately bad and that the world is a terrible place.

I watched a movie the other day about the Protestants and Catholics in Ireland. They were killing each other over the route that some of the children were taking to school. In my early years, growing up in Belfast I understand the history and thank God I was not raised to hate the other side. What difference does it make about which route innocent children walk to earn their education? If someone can answer these questions in a way that makes sense, then maybe I'll be satisfied. Some people say "an eye for an eye" but really where does it stop? An eye for an eye makes the whole world blind, as Ghandi said.

What's the use in working so much, to acquire all this money if you never have the time to take a vacation? If we're always planning ahead to what we will do next year, or when we will re-tire, because we don't have the time now, then we're really miss-ing out on what's happening right NOW. How much money does it take before people are really happy? If you suddenly had all the money in the world, would it make you happy? What is the first thing you would buy? What is the first thing you would give away? What are the three most important things in your life right now and how much do they cost?

To answer my own questions... if I was solely focused on mak-ing money for my retirement and forgetting to enjoy the present moment, then I'd be missing out on a lot of experiences. The past and future are important, but all I really have is right now. I know that if I had all the money in the world, it would not be the primary source of my happiness. If I suddenly won the lottery I *would buy a round-the-world plane ticket to meet people of different cultures and beliefs in the hopes of better understanding human nature. I would give away everything I owned, except maybe my photos. If money could buy freedom from oppression, then I'd invest in that. The three most important things in my life are: family, friendship, and love, total cost = $0.*

June 15, 2002 was one particularly frustrating day after watching coverage about the wars in Rwanda and the Congo. I was focused on problems, not solutions, and anger was just one sign of my discord with the world. There would be many more journal entries like that in the months to come.

There are Five Fallacies about Life that likewise create crisis, violence and killing, and war. First, the idea that human beings are separate from each other. Second, the idea that there is not enough of what human beings need to be happy. Third, the idea that in order to get the stuff of which there is not enough, human beings must compete with each other. Fourth, the idea that some human beings are better than other human beings. Fifth, the idea that it is appropriate for human beings to resolve severe differences created by all the other fallacies by killing each other. You think you are being terrorized by other people, but in truth you are being terrorized by your beliefs. [1]

– Neale Donald Walsch

---

1   *What God Said*, Neale Donald Walsch , page 10.

The world gone mad

Not only was I pissed off at the world, now I know that I was also attempting to deal with my own feelings of frustration and a general disconnection from the world around me. I wasn't buying into what I was hearing on the news every day. Yes I knew that bad things happened but I wasn't convinced that the world was a horrible place and that most people were bad.

In my early years in Belfast I knew even as a child that the Protestants were not above the Catholics and vice versa. Not everyone shared my views; thankfully I was raised to think for myself. I thought it was total insanity that in many places around the world people were still bombing and shooting each other over land claims or because of a different choice of religion, different skin colour, or insert whatever reason you can think of that separates us. Growing up in Canada I was exposed to a more diverse culture in the bigger cities; one that generally embraced the diversity of people, religion and ethnicity.

In 2002 living in Ottawa I had finished university and was working in a good job, I lived in nice apartment and had many friends – so I should have had nothing to complain about, right?

> **Reflection:**
> *Take a few moments to think about what angers or upsets you with the state of the world today?*

Numbing myself with distractions

I was stuck in a state of comparing myself to others at work. I was performing the same job as some of my peers, yet I knew I was getting paid less for it. I was feeling tired; I wasn't sleeping well. I was also suffering from frequent headaches. I even went to a doctor who prescribed me anti-depressants because he thought that it might relieve the headaches and help me get a better quality of sleep. Instead I ended up more restless and after a week of insomnia I quit taking the pills. But I kept on going through life and after a couple of years I left my job, moved from Ottawa to Toronto and decided to start over.

More and more signs of discord started to appear, manifesting as apathy towards work and a few too many late nights out drinking and partying during the week. After a year and a half I left my job, and decided to move across the country to the west coast of Canada, starting over once again.

I kept repeating this pattern in different cities and different jobs. Over the period of six years I moved from Ottawa to Victoria, back to Ottawa, then to Toronto. After a year and half in Toronto I moved to Vancouver with Adam. I was always excited to start a new job as it came with new challenges and meeting new people. However after about a year I had reached the top of my learning curve in each job; I no longer found the work challenging and I became bored. I left Vancouver when I broke off the relationship with Adam in 2006, and returned to London, Ontario when I finally reached my breaking point at work. For three consecutive months I was working 60-70 hour weeks. I was only home on the weekends when I would mostly sleep as I was too tired to socialize, I was having a few glasses of wine most nights of the week and I was exhausted. I was feeling out of balance and something had to give.

Enough was enough. There had to be more to life than what I was experiencing! There had to be a way where I could earn a living and live a balanced life. There had to be somewhere for me to work where I felt I was really making a difference. There had to be a way to find something I could do that I could be proud of, where I could channel my feelings of anger about the state of the world and actually do something about it. That was around the time I began enquiring about yoga teacher training programs, in the summer of 2008. It took a long time for me to realize that changing my outside circumstances, by moving to another city and getting another job, was not going to solve my problems, it was only when I began to look deeply within that things started to shift.

Your discordant mirror world

The world is like a mirror and it has a wonderful way of reflecting back at you what you are putting out there. During the years leading up to my breaking point, the fact that I was becoming increasingly more dissatisfied with my work and kept changing jobs was a sign to look in the mirror at what I was doing and if it was truly making me happy. I didn't have the awareness then to stop and examine why I kept moving around and leaving jobs behind. I thought that it was purely because I loved travel and adventure. While I do love travel and adventure, now I know that I was not fully using my talents of being able to help others to reach their full potential in a way that made me feel truly happy and satisfied. To get there, I had to learn to look in the mirror to notice the little things that upset me during the day—and reflect on why they irritated me. I'm sure you can relate.

Discord is defined as a lack of agreement between two people, or with oneself, or disconnection, strife, friction, hostility, conflict, bad feeling and apathy. This could show up in your life as feelings of isolation or loneliness, frustration or anger at the world around you and a general criticism of everything. The signs could show up as a minor irritation or they could manifest into a major personal issue. No matter what the signs are, experiencing discord with yourself usually means you are disconnected from your true nature; something is out of alignment.

Have you noticed how on a day where you spill coffee on yourself first thing in the morning, when you let that bother you, you can carry that energy with you throughout the day if you're not careful? For example, you might stub your toe on your way out the door, then you notice there are more angry drivers on the road than usual – one who has just cut you off, the person in front of you as you head into work, allowed the door to slam in your face, and nobody seems to be smiling on the street. Conversely, have you noticed on those mornings, when you walk out the door feeling good and with a smile on your face, that traffic seems to be flowing well, nobody is honking their horn and other people seem to be smiling and in a good mood too?

When you get to a point of awareness and understanding of what's really triggering you and stop taking other people's actions personally, you begin to realize that you have power over your emotions. Instead of lashing out at that careless driver who just cut you off, you can turn a potential volatile situation around in seconds, which in turn affects your day-to-day experience. It's helpful to practice changing your habits with small examples over time. Then, when it comes to dealing with a larger problem or with making a bigger change in life, you will already have built up helpful habits that will allow you to navigate life's bigger challenges with more ease.

How are you perpetuating unhappiness?

Unhappiness affects a lot of people and shows up in various forms. Common sources of unhappiness are money, work and relationships. Many years ago I experienced discord primarily in my work and relationships; there was a feeling of emptiness, of something missing but I didn't know then exactly what was missing.

Many of us strive for more - more money, more friends, a bigger house, a faster car, fancier clothes, etc. We get stuck comparing ourselves to others, or trying to impress and then come to the conclusion that we're not good enough. Therefore, we keep working harder and longer trying to make more money to get ahead.

There's nothing wrong with having ambition and in acquiring wealth in the form of more money or a beautiful home or a new car. You can have it all! But I'd like you to consider spiritual wealth or personal wellbeing as well. It's important to evaluate your intentions behind your desires and knowing how much is enough no matter what you are pursuing. For example, are you working so much that you are not spending enough time with your family or friends? Are you trying to fill an internal void with external luxuries?

If you're unaware of the intentions behind your desires, chances are you will always be striving for more and will rarely stop to appreciate what you have. When you come from a place of appreciation for what you already have, you're focusing on your strengths and celebrating your accomplishments. You are in a state of joy and gratitude, rather than a state of inadequacy or low self-worth.

What does your work mean to you?

Are you working to live or living to work? Is your work generally satisfying and enjoyable or do you often dread going to work? When someone asks you what you do, do you feel excited and proud to share your answer? These are important questions to ponder.

I was feeling bored and unfulfilled a lot of the time at work and I was getting frustrated with certain people whom I felt weren't listening to me or taking me seriously. Being a 25-year-old woman in a male dominated industry, managing people who were 10-15 years my senior came with its challenges. Instead of looking in the mirror to evaluate my contributions to the conflict in the workplace, I was focusing on what other people were doing wrong. Had I looked more closely at myself and my reactions, the experience could have been a lot less stressful.

Not only does it matter how often you're working but also how fulfilled you feel at the end of a day's work. I felt like I was doing well at work and I was good at my job but I wasn't feeling passionate about it, which left me feeling unfulfilled at the end of the day. People often say that when you've found your passion it doesn't feel like work and the days fly by. This doesn't mean that you will not face challenges. It's more about paying attention to how often challenges show up each day that cause you to feel anger or stress or fatigue, leaving you drained at the end of the day with little time for your family or social life. Maybe you are in the right line of work but your talents aren't being used to their fullest potential and you feel like you could be doing more in your current role.

If you don't take time to evaluate these questions you could be missing out on an opportunity to change your circumstances into a more fulfilling career that leaves you feeling happy and balanced at the end of the day.

Looking into your relationship mirror

A common source of unhappiness is reflected in relationships. Whenever conflict is experienced in a relationship with your intimate partner, your family, a friend or a work colleague, look closer at your own behaviour and how it contributes to the relationship. You may come to realize that you have an opportunity to change yourself, accept, or leave the situation, which puts you in a place of authentic personal power. While a certain element of conflict is normal and healthy, when dealt with consciously and respectfully in a relationship, continuous struggle and feelings of unhappiness are not normal.

I believe intimate relationships are like really big mirrors where we get to see and experience ourselves, our deepest insecurities, fears and dark emotions through the reflection of and our reaction to our partner's behaviour towards us. This brings these emotions to the surface and gives us a chance to heal the negative stuff that's not serving us.

Looking back, I believe I attracted an angry and verbally abusive partner into my life at that time so he could serve as a mirror for the some of the angry and aggressive behaviour I was putting out into the world. I wasn't walking around with a permanent frown and shouting at others all the time, but I was less conscious of other's feelings than I am now – I had no problems telling other people exactly what I thought of them, and with little tact.

I also believe we crossed paths so I could serve as his mirror to provide support to help him heal traumas of his past. Maybe there was more to it than that, but that's the most sense I can make out of the situation today. I also learned a very important lesson from that relationship – that I cannot fix or save anyone else and I am solely responsible for my own happiness and myself. I'm grateful for the good times and the hard times in my relationship with Adam, as the experience has made me a stronger person today.

If you find yourself struggling with frequent feelings of unhappiness in any area of your life; money, work or relationships, ask yourself three questions:

1. Can I continue to accept things as they are?
2. How could I change myself to respond differently?
3. Is my situation so unhealthy that I need to move on?

Knowing that you have choices puts you in the mindset of looking for solutions, instead of focusing on the problems of the other person, who you believe is causing you unhappiness. All of life is a mirror, where our inter- actions with others and our reactions to situations often say more about our internal state and ourselves in a given moment, than about the other person.

Experiencing the clouds of frustration

The path you take to happiness may be clouded by frustration, if you feel things are not going according to your plan and on your schedule. Frustra- tion in large doses can hurt you. It stems from your perception of your ability to overcome obstacles and can also be caused by conflict. It's ok to feel up- set or annoyed from time to time, however if it's a dominant feeling for you, it can affect your mental health and could manifest itself into chronic stress and anxiety. We'll cover more on that in Chapter 11 when learning about the wisdom of the body.

When you experience frustration you have a choice to react or respond to the circumstances causing the frustration. I have reacted frequently in the past in my personal and professional relationships and in that state I have missed the opportunity to learn about myself in that moment. Now that I know better, I realize that I always have the power to choose how to respond. When I'm experiencing frustration, I know it's time to step back from the situation to see what's really going on underneath my feelings of aggravation. Reacting through actions or words comes from a place of defensiveness, causing you to lash out, often with a loss of control, which can escalate a situation and have you say things you may regret later. Responding by taking a mindful approach to pause, become aware of your emotional state and think about what you will say is more thoughtful and usually leads to a more positive outcome.

Boredom and apathy

Other signs of discord are boredom and apathy. I attribute boredom to procrastination or a lack of decision. Apathy surfaces when one is feeling hopeless or has lost faith in him or herself. I reached the peak of boredom and frustration at work, which turned to apathy in my career in the summer of 2008. I felt that all I was doing was working and performing the same tasks over and over again, even though the clients would vary. I was living to work and had an unhealthy balance between my work and social life. I have always held myself to high standards, yet I was starting to care less about my performance at work and was daydreaming a lot about what else I could be doing with my life. Finally the daydreaming led me to start taking action and I began talking to my close friends about my feelings and desires to do something different.

Taking action and following a plan can tackle both boredom and apathy, or by changing your plan if the one you have is not working. Temporary states of boredom or apathy are expected in one's life – if you are experiencing these feelings often or consistently, to the point where you are feeling generally disengaged with your surroundings, it's time to take action to get unstuck. This might even mean seeking out professional help.

You may be experiencing other signs of discord that I haven't yet touched upon and we'll explore solutions more in-depth throughout this book. Now it's time to explore your current state. Remember when freewriting or brainstorming, don't worry about spelling or grammar or how your journal might sound if someone were to read it. It's personal to you, try to let go of any judgment of what you're writing and don't worry about the outcome.

Exercise: Explore Your Current State

For a minimum of one week, spend time getting to know your inner world through freewriting for five to ten minutes a day. I encourage you to try this for at least one week in order to get into the habit of daily writing. If you are able to continue journaling for the time that you are reading this book, it will be helpful for you to go back and reflect upon your state at different stages of your journey. The frustrations that you are experiencing today might be quite different than the ones you are facing by the time you are finished the book.

1. **Make a commitment to yourself**
   Today is the perfect day to start. It's the first step on your journey. You can't get this wrong and you can always go back to revisit and elaborate on your writing at the end of the week. Say it out loud: "I _____, commit to spending _____ minutes each day to freewriting, for seven days." Write this down on the first page of your journal, sign it and date it.

2. **Find a consistent time each day and a place where it will be quiet so you can focus**
   This could be first thing in the morning before everyone else wakes up and before you start going about your day. If you're a night owl then set aside time in the evening. Consistency is key.

3. **Don't allow yourself to get distracted**
   Your household chores, phone and cat can wait. We're very good at creating distractions when we don't want to do something, even if it's for our greater good. For example, my apartment was always spotless right before exam time in school! If you really can't help

yourself, then get all of those distractions out of the way today: clean your house, run your errands and then start writing.

4. **Take a few moments to relax yourself before you begin.** Whether that's sitting quietly, taking a few deep breaths, or making a cup of tea to accompany you while you write, make this part of your daily ritual.

5. **Forget about the outcome**

   Don't worry about your writing style or spelling, as you won't be sharing this with anyone. Don't be afraid of what might be revealed for fear of uncovering your deepest, darkest secrets, or fear of offending someone. This is a process of self discovery and the point of this exercise is get you in the habit of taking action and to begin to release your inner thoughts onto paper, to see what lies underneath and for reflection later on.

If you're stuck for inspiration, start by writing out a question or a statement you've been pondering, or think about how any of the signs of discord show up in your life, and then allow your pen to reveal the answers through your writing.

Sometimes it's enough to get the creative juices flowing to describe what you did the prior day or to write out what you are looking forward to today. I encourage you to come up with your own questions or statements. If you're feeling stuck, here are some examples of statements to help you get started:

1. The one thing that makes me feel sad is ____ (fill in the blank).
2. I would describe my perfect day as ____.
3. I feel most angry when ____.
4. Today I am most looking forward to ____.
5. I feel most happy when I am ____.

At the end of the seven days, go back and read what you have written and notice if you spot any patterns in your writing. Silence the inner critic and do not be concerned about spelling or grammar or if the words even make sense. Imagine looking at the content objectively as if you are reading someone else's words.

1. Is there something there that you have written about more than once that may be trying to get your attention?
2. Are there any particular words that jump out at you?
3. Write down what you notice.

If you really enjoyed this exercise, I recommend you continue freewriting daily for the entire time you are reading this book or even longer, as it helps to unload the mind first thing in the morning or at the end of the day. If you didn't enjoy this exercise, I also recommend that you continue freewriting daily for the entire time you are reading this book. We often resist the things we most need to learn or change about ourselves. Maybe you can write about why you don't like freewriting.

Chapter Three Find Your Tribe

- October 9, 2008 – The real journey begins

After eight hours on the bus we have finally arrived at the Anand Prakash Ashram in Rishikesh. Thankfully I had a fairly uneventful arrival at the airport in Delhi. I think I was anticipating more chaos, however I managed to exchange money, flag a taxi and get myself to the hotel without incident. My first exposure to Delhi traffic was exhilarating, scary and amusing all at once. The taxi driver was really quiet but his horn, along with the honking of the other cars and trucks as they were weaving in and out and dodging people, cows and dogs, was not so quiet. He had his left hand on the wheel to steer and his right hand on the horn the whole time. I suppose after driving around in that madness day after day you would become oblivious to the constant noise. I was amazed at the order that was created out of chaos on the roads. It seems there are no rules or lines to divide the lanes, never mind the additional worry about avoiding hitting a person, a dog, or God forbid, a cow.

The ashram is a little piece of heaven tucked up here in the foothills of the Himalayas, where I'll be spending the next five weeks immersing myself in yoga and meditation and soaking up Indian culture. Not only have I arrived physically but I have a feeling this is where the real journey begins where I get to explore more about myself.

- October 15, 2008 – Day three of the course

We've been in Rishikesh for one week already. The first few days getting up at 5:30 am for morning practice were a struggle, mostly due to jetlag, but now I've settled into a nice routine.

I've met some wonderful people from all over the world and together we're learning a lot. It's a mix of philosophy, asana practice, teaching one-on-one and techniques class where we are learning appropriate language and cues when guiding a yoga class. I've discovered that even though I've been practicing yoga for ten years now, there are still a few postures that I have been doing incorrectly, so it's comforting to learn the right way, finally. Our teachers, Vishva and Chetana, have put together a full program and I have a feeling I will take away much more than just learning the content.

This morning in class I was in the front row looking at the mountains and listening to the group chant and I had the all-familiar déjà vu feeling. It was like I had imagined or dreamt about this place before. Small tears of happiness began to trickle down my cheeks – I felt completely content and was sure I was exactly where I was meant to be at that moment. I closed my eyes and sat still in meditation for the longest time in my life so far. I lost the sounds around me and slipped into my interior world and felt a slight tingling sensation on my forehead. Then I saw some pretty interesting visuals inside my head – it was like a movie and I'm not sure if I can do it justice by writing alone, maybe painting a picture would help? It was like a vortex, or at least that's how it started off, then there was a white/grey coloured jellyfish-like im-

age that pulsated in and out, more of a cross between a jellyfish with squid legs, then suddenly a kaleidoscope image appeared in its place. This was soon replaced by a dark pool and I saw a snake and some other random images – a diamond-shaped pendant, a Celtic knot and purplish stones with circles swirling on the out-side. Everything was moving in my mind as I sat so very still. Is this what meditation is all about? Is this what it means to reach a higher state of consciousness? I suppose I'm not going to be an expert at meditation right away, they say it takes practice!

- October 19, 2008 – Sunday, a day off!

It's Sunday evening after dinner we have been up since 5:30 a.m. for self-practice, followed by an 18-kilometer walk and an hour and a half of practice teaching yoga. I feel so energized. I also managed to squeeze a massage into my day and did a bit of shopping for the essentials, toilet paper and shampoo. I final-ly tried the hot chilli chocolate everyone has been talking about and it's amazing. That could be part of the reason I'm feeling charged up, but I think most of the rush is coming from the prac-tice teaching earlier.

We had a group of six and we each went through the sun sal-utation series and one other pose. The feedback was invaluable and I feel so excited about teaching - I can only see it getting better from here. I think the vegetarian diet is also helping as I feel better stronger and I feel less hungry between meals, per-haps my sugar levels are more balanced now. I'm not having as many highs and lows and near panic attacks when my sugar level drops - must incorporate these good habits into my daily life when I return. It's easy to slip back into old habits and make promises of changing, but this time it feels different, it's like a

43

new commitment to ME. Happy Sunday, what a beautiful day!

- October 27, 2008 – Diwali celebrations

We've just finished our first test on the course and I have confidence that it went really well. It's Diwali, the festival of light, which seems to be equivalent to New Year's Eve back home with the excitement in the village. We'll be indulging in lots of celebrations including sweets and fireworks tonight and tomorrow. It's also the one-year anniversary of the ashram tomorrow so it's really special that we are here to celebrate all of this together. We've been told there is a 100-year old yogi coming tomorrow to teach morning class. I wonder if he will put all of us to shame with his skills.

In this afternoon's class earlier, Vishva suggested that we just let things go, especially tonight, given that it's New Year and New Moon. I can think of a few things to release, starting with sad feelings over old relationships. I'm ready to open up my heart up again and see what happens. I'm grateful for all experiences that are coming to me, as they are an opportunity to learn. This new way of thinking I've acquired over the past few weeks does tend to make life seem easier. I've connected with some wonderful souls and I feel like I have a new family. People have shared their vulnerability, which has made it a bit easier for me to start sharing mine – something I've always kept a tight lid on. I'm remembering our chant from kirtan the other night:

Om Sarve Bhavantu Sukhinah
Sarve Santu Nir-Aamayaah
Sarve Bhadraanni Pashyantu
Maa Kashcid-Duhkha-Bhaag-Bhavet

Om Shaantih Shaantih Shaantih

Which means:
Om, May All become Happy,
May All be Free from Illness.
May All See what is Auspicious,
May no one Suffer.
Om Peace, Peace, Peace.

Finding your tribe

During my first visit to India, as I was learning more about myself and my inner world through meditation, I was also finding and connecting with my tribe. The people on my course seemed so friendly and loving, even though we didn't know each other at first, and it didn't take long to form close friendships. We bonded because we shared similar experiences with many of us leaving behind family and friends and a job to take the five-week immersion into yoga in a land that was far from home. Many of us were dealing with personal struggles. Some of us wanted to become yoga teachers, while others were looking to deepen their personal practice. The common thread that drew us together was a desire for personal growth and healing, even if we didn't recognize the desire right away.

While we were living in a communal environment there was still enough time to be alone, allowing for self-reflection. I wrote in my journal at length each morning after yoga class. We observed *mauna* (or silence) in the ashram every night beginning at 9 pm until after breakfast. This allowed me plenty of time to dwell in my thoughts, thoughts about my prior romantic relationships, and lack of, kept reoccurring. I was feeling angry with myself for letting Adam hurt me in the way that I allowed him to. The nagging thoughts kept replaying in my mind – I'm so smart, I've done well in school, I've always managed to land a job, I have a good family, I'm a strong person, yet how could I allow someone to be verbally abusive towards me? How could I put up with that for so long and not tell anyone?

Imagine this going through my mind only to be contrasted with hearing the words from Vishva in class that as our true selves we are love, we are joyful and playful and fearless. It was getting easier each day to not let the negative thoughts dominate my day, especially amidst the celebration of light and dancing around Diwali celebrations. I often felt like I was on an emotional roller coaster. There were times when I felt stupid and selfish knowing that there were so many greater problems in the world than my personal struggles. Somehow being able to isolate myself from my friends and family in the ashram and share some of my experiences with my new tribe was helping me to heal – helping me to get back to being my true self – joyful, playful and fearless.

Experiencing discomfort with your current circles

When you are on a journey of personal growth you might find that you've been outgrowing certain experiences lately. You may be questioning some of your friendship circles, your job or even your romantic relationships. Feeling discomfort in these areas is okay: it's a sign that you may need to evaluate your current company and determine if changes need to be made to your 'tribe'.

Your 'tribe' is your people - kindred spirits who understand and connect with the authentic you. They are people who share your vision and you may come together in a community to connect, support, inspire, and hold each other accountable to help you become your best self-possible. This could be your family or best friend, but it doesn't have to be. It could be someone you've met where you share a common interest. I was able to connect with and identify with people who shared my love of yoga and desire for personal development. With social media and the Internet, we live in a global village and you can find your tribe anywhere.

You've probably heard the saying "we're all in this together and nobody is getting out alive!" As humans, it's inherent in our nature to connect. It's right up there with our need for food and water. Studies have been done and the data suggests that we are shaped by our social environment and we are affected when our social bonds are threatened or non-existent.

> **Reflection:**
> *Think about who you have in your social circles today. If you were to share your dreams with some of these people, what do you think they would say?*

Start with where you are

My tribe was presented to me when I landed in India to embark upon my yoga teacher training with a group of people who came from all over the world. At that time I wasn't actively seeking them out. What drew us together at that particular point in time in that place was a desire for personal growth and healing. I was looking for something but I wasn't sure then what it was; I only knew at the time that I was feeling stressed out and disconnected from the life that I had created. I was pondering life's big questions about why I was here and what my purpose was on earth. While I didn't instantly bond with everyone on the course, there were a few people who I became quite close to rather quickly. We enjoyed each other's company outside of our studies. We were able to have deep and meaningful conversations together, revealing personal details about our lives that we normally wouldn't reveal to strangers. We laughed a lot together.

I'm still in touch with some people from my time in India and my tribe has evolved over time. The more I get to know myself and get clearer on my values, the more people keep showing up in my life that reflect my current values. Not only have I maintained friendships from my time in India, now I'm surrounded by a supportive group of social entrepreneurs through my co-working space in downtown Vancouver.

When seeking out your tribe, start with where you are now – do you have any current friends or family members who share your dreams and vision? Can you imagine any of them supporting you or holding you accountable with what you wish to achieve? If you answered, yes, then you're off to a great start. Maybe you are in a position to offer support or to mentor others and connecting with your community is your way of giving back to further uplift others. Even if you're here as a mentor or teacher, you will learn so much from connecting to others who are on a similar path – everyone can be a teacher.

Get to know your local community

If you're feeling alone in your quest and don't have family or friends who share your passions and who you feel you can connect with, then start to look around in your community for inspiration. This could be in your physical community – your neighbourhood, town or city, or in an online community related to topics that interest or excite you. For example, now that I'm living in Vancouver and I'm interested in social entrepreneurship, I've joined a local learning and support group of social entrepreneurs who meet once per month to exchange ideas, share knowledge and support each other's growth. Each month, we meet for a potluck dinner where afterwards, one of us has the chance to facilitate a group discussion on a topic that we have expertise in. This not only allows us to get feedback on the latest projects we're working on, but also offers the opportunity to ask for support from the group.

With the awareness of what brings you joy and with the intent of connection, start paying attention to bulletin boards at your local school, community centre or library, start sharing your ideas and notice your conversations and connections with acquaintances or strangers and see what comes up. It only takes one person to take that first step to reach out and before you know it, you will start to expand your social and professional networks with the people who are here to help you on your journey. You may not identify and connect with everyone whom you come across, and that's okay. What's important is that you pay attention to those people who you feel good around, people who lift you up and support you, and whom you may be able to offer inspiration and support to in return.

Quite often the answers we are looking for are right in front of us and are offered up by way of synchronicity; you will notice if you are paying attention to the signs. Synchronicity was first described by the psychiatrist Carl Jung, as a concept when multiple events that occur that seem to have no causal relationship, yet they are somehow, meaningfully connected. For example, a chance meeting with a stranger in a coffee shop who notices the book you are reading and strikes up a conversation with you. She happens to be in the same field of work or study as you and ends up becoming your mentor.

For me, my encounter with synchronicity happened during a conversation with my sister one night when I was sharing my desires to pursue yoga teacher training, she casually mentioned that I should talk to her cousin-in-law, Susheela, who had just returned from an ashram in India. Susheela had spent six weeks living in the communal ashram environment, or spiritual hermitage, and had obtained her 200-hour yoga teacher training certificate. I called Susheela the next day. It was only a few minutes into our conversation that I blurted out "I'm going." Susheela said 'but you don't know anything about the place.' It didn't matter, I had made my decision. When I later got to India I learned that Vishva and Chetana spent half their year in Ottawa and half in Rishikesh and that we had a friend in common – my very first yoga teacher in Ottawa, named Barry! Synchronicity in action - it's a small world.

With these suggestions, it's important to consider that it's not about the quantity of people you are connecting with, rather the *quality* of the relationships you are cultivating. You should pay attention to how you feel when you start to spend time with new people – maybe they are your tribe, or maybe they have appeared to show you what you don't want – either way, you will benefit from each experience.

Connecting with your tribe and identifying with others who are on a similar path is an important part of your growth and transformation, because you have people there to support you on those days where you might be feeling overwhelmed or tired and are in need of a dose of inspiration. We all have something to offer. We often share many of the same struggles and when we come together as a community we share our wisdom to learn from one another and grow together.

Checking In:
How is your daily freewriting practice going in your journal? Have you been keeping up with writing, even if for a few minutes a day? If not, what do you think is stopping you from writing?

Exercise: Visualize Your Tribe

It's time to get out your journal for a quick exercise.

Before you go down the path of reaching out to your find your tribe, let's take some time to visualize the type of people you imagine surrounding yourself with. Whether you wish to brainstorm by writing a list, or continue with freewriting, is up to you.

1. With a gentle smile on your face, close your eyes and take a few deep breaths. Think of a time when you felt on top of the world, when you felt fully supported and free to express the real you, without any judgment. As you breathe in, allow that feeling to expand throughout your body and enjoy the expansion it brings. As you breathe out, allow your body to become more relaxed.

2. If nothing comes to mind, use your imagination to feel what it would be like to be totally free and happy and surrounded by people who support you in your growth.

3. After a few minutes, or when it feels right, open your eyes and write down some of the sensations you felt in your body, what images or words came to mind during that exercise.

4. Go a little deeper and describe the qualities of the person, or people, who were there with you during the visualization. By performing this visualization you are calling into existence your future tribe.

Now it's time to take action. What's the first smallest step you can take to seek out and connect with your tribe? I challenge you take this first step within one week from today.

Chapter Four

- November 5, 2008 – Receiving my name

As the yoga course has come to a close, we had our name ceremony last night. On the card I received it read:

Dear Sarah,

Your spiritual name is 'Shobhana' - representing light. May your inner light guide you and help you to inspire your students. This name reminds me of Siobhan and the connections with yoga and Celtic wisdom.

~ Chetana and Yogi Vishvketu

Earlier that day we created a vision board, by cutting out various images and words from magazines, gluing them onto a piece of bristol board and decorating with colourful markers and string. Basically anything we could find, as supplies were somewhat limited. I was drawn to images of beautiful places, I also included an airport and backpack – travel is definitely on my horizon! I will keep the spirit of the fireworks, dancing and music we experienced over Diwali in my mind as I go. Life is a celebration, let the journey continue…

Seeing myself in a new light

The five weeks on the teacher training went by quickly and I went through a transformation; I was introduced to a new way of seeing myself and my place in the world. In the weeks that followed the training, traveling around on my own in India helped me to transition from the structured life I had created to the nomadic one I was living at that time. Being in a state of transition helped me to see that the future was full of opportunity and it was up to me to create it.

I was beginning to see my career in a more positive light and was appreciating my past accomplishments. I was thinking more about the good times I had with my coworkers, rather than focusing on the negative aspects of feeling stressed and being overworked. I could see a vision of my future where I got to choose which projects I wanted to work on and where I would be able to travel and teach yoga around the world.

I was starting to appreciate that the world wasn't a terrible place after all, probably because I hadn't watched the news in well over a month – I was living in my own happy bubble. The idea that I am not made up of the stories that play over and over again in my mind and I am not my past stuck with me. It helped me to see that I can recreate myself at any time and I am not bound to my history, which made the idea of the future feel limitless. I experienced kindness from strangers, most of whom had little to offer in the way of wealth, yet I was welcomed into people's homes; people who didn't know anything about me.

One woman who was particularly impactful on me was Meenakshi, who lived in a little blue house in one of the back alleys on the way from the ashram to the market in Rishikesh. I walked this back alley path almost daily and at the front of the blue house was Meenakshi's tiny store called the Jagriti Women's Centre. It was run by Meenakshi and her family where she sold handicrafts made from women in remote villages in the Himalayas. She delivered the profits back to the women as this was their main source of income for survival. The handmade notebooks in her store caught my attention the first time I walked by and I purchased one to use as a journal. We instantly became friends and I was invited in for chai and biscuits.

During the time I was there I got to know her whole family and was often invited in for lunch where she would share her dreams about how she wanted to expand her business to help more women. Her instant kindness and acceptance of me into her family struck me. I will always remember her commitment to help the women in her native village in the mountains.

On my last day in Rishikesh shortly after the course had ended, I decided to order her business cards so she could start handing them out in the market to attract more people to her store. I was in such a rush to pack up and catch my train to Delhi that I asked Pramod, the ashram office manager at the time, to please make sure the cards were delivered to the blue house in the alley when they arrived from the printer as I wouldn't be there to deliver them myself. I wasn't sure if they would make it but had to hope for the best. Sometimes you have to have faith that things will work out, even if you can't see it at the time.

You are pure potential

When I left India I felt like I was heading in the direction of my full potential. I knew then I had the capacity to make a difference in people's lives, helping them to relax through teaching yoga, even if I didn't know all of the details about what my full potential was at that time. I was feeling much more joy and freedom, connection with my new friends and fellow travelers and a lot less frustration day to day. By taking some time to reach out and help someone else, by ordering the business cards for Meenakshi, I had hoped that I was contributing to the growth of her business, even if only in a small way.

Explore your dreams

I have big dreams now. I've accomplished a lot so far and yet some days

I feel like I'm just getting started. New ideas are coming to me often and I believe I'm capable of making anything happen. During my first trip to India I had a dream that I would return one day to bring a group on a yoga retreat. I wanted them to experience a little piece of the ashram life that I had enjoyed, and possibly some personal growth at the same time. That dream came to life just three years later in 2011 when my retreat partner, Barb, and I brought a group for a two-week retreat of yoga, hiking and sightseeing.

My big dream now is to reach many people through the writing of this book – to serve as an inspiration and to encourage you to look within to find your gifts that you were meant to bring to the world. When you think about something you wish to change or accomplish in your life, it's important to have dreams or an end goal in mind, and it's equally important to break it down into manageable steps, to take action, and find ways to enjoy the process – after all, part of the journey is to reclaim our true nature of joy and bliss.[1]

Reflection:
As a child, do you remember anyone asking you what kind of person you wanted to be when you grew up? Not necessarily what you wanted to do for work but 'who' you wanted to be?

Your dreams are what you make them

Your dreams are important and they can be big or small to you. Sometimes people dream big then think it's too much to achieve; they don't know where to start and therefore give up before they begin. Others may have a dream but think it's not important enough, or are afraid of upsetting family or friends, so they don't bother going after it. If your dreams are wild and crazy

---

1   Inspired by the words of my teacher, Yogrishi Vishvketu.

and you believe you will fulfill them, you will. If your dreams are just within your reach and you believe it's not possible to fulfill them, you won't. Either way, whatever you believe, you are right.

Your beliefs become your thoughts,
Your thoughts become your words,
Your words become your actions,
Your actions become your habits,
Your habits become your values,
Your values become your destiny.
- Mahatma Ghandi

Ghandi said it very well. Your beliefs and thoughts typically become a self-fulfilling prophecy. There is a continuous feedback loop between your beliefs and thoughts, which tends to influence your actions, whether positive or negative in nature. Repeated actions become habits, which in turn affect your day-to-day life. For example if you are the person who has a dream in mind but believes it's too big to pursue or you fear upsetting your family then chances are you will not take the steps to make your dream come to life. You may tell people that you're too old or it's too late to try something new, you have too many responsibilities and that other people are depending on you. Therefore you continue on with life, perhaps thinking of your dream from time to time but making sure you tell yourself it's too crazy to pursue each time it comes up. Your destiny then becomes one where you settle, never taking the chance or dedicating the time to properly try to reach your full potential. You may be ok with this or you may be left with a feeling of a void or "what if?"

As Walt Disney said, "If you can dream it, you can do it." If you are day-dreaming about your future, it's important to pay attention to what you're thinking about. It's also wise to notice when the mind is playing tricks on you by imposing fear or doubt. We'll expand more upon breaking through fear and doubt in Chapter 7. For now, let's stay with your dreams.

Tapping into your subconscious mind

When you are thinking about what you wish to bring into your life and digging deeper into your dreams, much of this is done on the conscious level. Often it's not just your conscious awareness that shapes your dreams and desires. Tapping into your subconscious mind is one way to get in touch with what's really driving you. You can explore your subconscious mind in a variety of ways; some of which we are exploring in this book through meditation, freewriting, and journaling. Another way is by examining your night-time dreams.

Have you kept a dream journal?

Have you ever struggled with a complex problem at work to find yourself waking up in the middle of the night with a solution or an idea? I often wake up in the middle of the night with new ideas that I want to write about. I keep a pen and notebook by my bed so I can take notes, then go back to sleep.

A dream journal is a tool that can be used to tap into the subconscious mind, providing you with insights into your inner world helping you to solve problems that your conscious mind is not able to easily address. In our ever-increasing busy world, what you are not able to process during the day often finds its way into your dreams at night. Taking notice of what's happening in your mind while sleeping is another way of connecting into your inner being to receive information.

The next time you wake up from a recurring dream, write down what happened and put your conscious mind into a state of inquiry by asking what your subconscious mind is trying to tell you. Freewriting may reveal the answer.

A tale of two cities

When I was traveling for a few months in Southeast Asia, I used to waste a lot of time obsessing over where I would settle down when I returned to Canada or thinking about if I should settle down in Canada. I kept a dream journal and over the course of a few weeks, each night before I went to bed I would ask that I be able to remember my dreams in the morning. Making this statement out loud encourages the subconscious mind to cooperate.

I had a recurring dream of getting on a bus, being somewhat lost and not able to get off at my stop. Two cities, Ottawa and Toronto, that I had lived in previously, were predominant in my dreams, yet I was not able to get off the bus in these cities. I took this to mean that I was not meant to return to either of them to live. A few weeks later I came to the conclusion that I did not have to decide where I was going to settle down and that I was meant to keep on traveling for the time being. The recurring bus dreams stopped after that.

Reflecting upon this, it's almost amusing to think that my subconscious mind was sending a message to say thank you to my conscious mind for coming to a conclusion and to stop obsessing about the future. The more I was worrying about the future and where I might live, the more vivid the bus dreams became. When I let go of the indecision on the conscious level, the unconscious mind was also cleared. I never did return to Ottawa or Toronto to live.

Exercise: Define Your Dreams

With your journal nearby, revisit and write responses to similar questions that you were reflecting upon earlier. Notice if anything is getting in the way of your writing, such as a tiny voice that's telling you it's not possible, or that your dreams are crazy. The more you pay attention to the voices in your head, the more you will begin to decipher between those voices that are there to encourage you and those that are peppered with doubt. Try to ignore the negative, doubtful voices and keep writing.

1. What are your dreams?
2. Imagine there are no limits and you can pursue anything, what would it be?
3. What legacy do you wish to leave behind?
4. What is preventing you from taking the first step?

Chapter Five INTENTIONS

- November 11, 2008 – On the road again

It's Remembrance Day and I'm on the plane sitting in seat 18a, waiting to take off to head to Chennai. I have just finished reading some of Deepak Chopra's sutras in 'The Path to Love' book and thought I would choose three that resonate with me at the moment.

- *Love dances in the freshness of the unknown.*
- *Love grows on the basis of giving.*
- *You will be in love when you know that you are love.*

Chopra also talks about the chakras, energy centres of the body, which we explored in the teacher training. The higher chakras are for will, intuition and freedom, and the lower chakras are about survival, sexual drive and power. If only we humans lived in the higher three, we would see ourselves as divine and we might never go to war, create enemies, or struggle for survival. The heart is at the centre – it's the mediator that uses our centre of feeling where we have the rhythm of every intimate relationship, dancing between risk and retreat. Over and over we repeat this rhythm accepting love and pushing it away until finally something miraculous happens one day and we recognize that we are all light and we stop pushing love away. Chopra says it so well. I'm finally on my own in India, at least for the next few hours, as I will be meeting Sathya's family later today. Sathya and I used to work together in London and her brother lives in Chennai. How amazing is it to have connections all over the world! Now that I'm traveling alone, I'm looking forward to further contemplation and to integrate the plethora of knowledge from the past month. Vishva and Chetana said it could take a few months to fully absorb the teachings.

My intentions:
- *To explore love from within. Apparently there's a wellspring in there just waiting to burst – at least that's what I took away from the yoga teacher training.*
- *Find a place to teach yoga when I arrive in Edinburgh.*
- *Land an amazing short-term contract that pays really well, so I may continue my travels and teach yoga in different countries.*
- *I also intend to finish this delicious masala dosa that is in front of me, who knew plane food could be so tasty?*

- November 13, 2008 – The fisherman and Santana's restaurant

This is only the third time in five weeks that I've experienced rain in India. I had a lovely morning walking around The Pancha (Five) Rathas here in Mahabalipuram. One of my favourite carvings was an elephant, of course. Then I went the Shore Temple and finally dipped my feet in the Bay of Bengal. As I was wandering through a back alley I stumbled upon an entrance to the beach and came across Santana's restaurant where I'm now sitting in my prime patio seat to people-watch, read and write.

61

I've picked up the God of Small Things by Arundhati Roy and am looking forward to spending the afternoon relaxing and sipping on my mango lassi. Bliss.

I've just had a conversation with the waiter as he sat down at my table and wanted to know where I was from and what I was doing here. I asked him why there seemed to be so many people on the beach that day crowded at the water's edge. He went on to explain that yesterday morning the men had gone out fishing in their colourful long fishing boats, as they normally do each day, however the water was very rough and one of the boats capsized. Unfortunately one of the men had caught his leg in the fishing net and was trapped underneath the boat. The other three men and the boat made it back to shore but the fourth man, who was caught, sadly drowned.

Before I sat down here at the restaurant I had taken a few photos, was admiring my view and the vibrant colours of the women's saris, thinking how perfect of a day it was. I didn't realize they were gathered there to mourn. The waiter had a big grin on his face, which confused me, given the circumstances. I asked if he felt sad by what happened and if he knew the man who died. He said he did and it was not a problem that he died since that was God's will, but the real problem is he has three young children and now they are left without a father. That statement has stopped me in my tracks and now I feel guilty for taking photos. I'm thinking about mum and dad and my sisters, Jenny and Rachel. I can't imagine losing my dad at a young age, how different life would have been. I don't think I can focus on reading now; it's time to just stare at the water and continue to take in my surroundings and appreciate what I have.

After zoning out or being present, whatever it was, observing my surroundings has helped me realize that my appreciation for what I have and where I am right now is coming from my heart, I felt a physical twinge in there and I don't really know where the last half hour has gone. Time to go for a walk...

- November 14, 2008 – More about love

Right now, at this moment, I feel truly happy and at peace with myself and I realize all prior experiences, whether good or bad, have simply prepared me for this point in my life. It's been said that you get back what you put out there and it's true, I'm ready to put myself and my heart out there and experience all that the world has to offer and all that love has to teach me. It's amazing how a mere thought can manifest itself in so many ways in the universe – now to keep working on not getting caught up in my thoughts and to be open to the opportunities that come my way. What an amazing day.

Thoughts and intentions

After five weeks of intense study I was ready to transition from the happy ashram bubble of life back into the real world. I was planning to travel around the south of India in Tamil Nadu and Kerala for a few weeks before heading to Edinburgh. During the journey on the plane from Delhi to Chennai I was contemplating the chakras and realized I had been living primarily in the lower three chakras (survival, sexual drive and power) for many years of my life. I felt like this was a transition time and I was looking forward to exploring more into the higher chakras (will, intuition, freedom and love) given that I got a taste of it during my training.

I was starting to trust more in the endless possibilities of my future knowing that I had the ability to create whatever life I wanted, even if I didn't know exactly how I would do it. While I had intentions of finding a job and teaching yoga when I arrived in Edinburgh, the old me would have been doing everything possible to make this happen while I was still traveling in India for those last few weeks. Instead the newer me decided to enjoy my vacation time and sort things out when I arrived in Edinburgh as it would all work out in due time. I embraced the surrender.

Surrender to your heart's desire

India has a way of making you surrender. It's a country of so many contrasts and contradictions, which can't be summed up in a few paragraphs. Even though it's busy and hot and often crazy, there always seems to be a divine order amidst the chaos – like the traffic I experienced on my first day in Delhi. No rules, no dividing lines on the road, yet everyone figures out how to get to their destination safely – everything has a way of just working out.

While I consider Edinburgh less chaotic than Delhi, things seemed to work out for me brilliantly when I landed there, even without me having to interfere with my future while I was still traveling in India. Within two weeks of arriving in Edinburgh I had landed a contract job and discovered a church hall to start up my own yoga classes. The church was only a five-minute walk from where I was living. I also took on my first private yoga clients; my cousin-in-law, Sigi and her sister Sonia. Sigi is a doctor with a demanding schedule and she was expecting her first son at that time. It was such a delight to go to her house each week to teach prenatal yoga, which was usually followed by a meal and a good natter (catch-up) as they say in Edinburgh.

Thoughts without intention are just thoughts and they will not materialize into anything without action. Intention is having aim or purpose; it's something you are meant to do - an imagined outcome that guides your actions. If you can imagine the outcome as already here, it fuels your intentions and actions with more power. I love how Wayne Dyer describes the co-creative process between the universe and us in his book, 'The Power of Intention.'

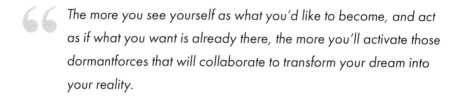 *The more you see yourself as what you'd like to become, and act as if what you want is already there, the more you'll activate those dormant forces that will collaborate to transform your dream into your reality.*

– Wayne Dyer

Having an intention and a vision of what you'd like to become or what you would like to achieve is a good place to start. When you incorporate as many of the five senses as possible into your vision and feel the emotions associated with your vision, it gives your intention more power.

Reflection:
Think of a place where you have always dreamed to vacation. Imagine yourself there. What does the place look like? What smells do you notice around you? What is the temperature? What sounds do you hear around you? What does the food taste like? How do you feel being there? Explore as many sensations as possible.

Whether you are visualizing going to a lush destination or dreaming of something you would like to create in your future, when you imagine your outcome as already here, it gives your idea more power. Paint a really clear picture in your mind of your heart's desire and take a few moments each day to experience it as if it were already here.

Balancing the scales of effort and allowing

Moving forward on your path is about finding the delicate balance between effort and allowing – setting your intention then taking action to make it happen, while appreciating what you already have – this will get you closer to your desired outcome.

I'm a very action-oriented person; I often make things happen by effort and sheer determination, however I've learned along the way that if I'm trying too hard to force an outcome that I'm actually going against the creative forces of the universe. As my dear friend Barb often says, "If you're working too hard, you're working too hard." Perhaps a simple and obvious statement, but it reminds me to slow down and shift my focus, when I feel frustrated with a lack of progress.

Some of the best things have often come to me with ease. The creation of the Helping Hands for India children's charity is a perfect example of an organization that was created with ease and without a major initial plan. The power was in me setting my intention to find a way to use my skills to make a difference in the lives of others, and then allowing the final results to be delivered when the time was right.

When a small group of yoga teachers first got together to create Helping Hands for India, initially I wanted to have a strategic plan in place, to have the operations of the charity defined and to know exactly where we would be with a five-year plan. I was advised by my teacher Vishva's mentor - a wise man called Swami Amlanand, who ran an ashram in nearby Haridwar - that things in India do not always work according to a defined plan. He suggested we start small and to see where it would lead. We started by setting up an official sponsorship program connecting sponsors and children, helping the children to attend school by paying for their basic needs, such as uniforms, books and school supplies. Over the years, with the support of the yoga community, our charity grew into much more than a sponsorship program, something I could not have predicted. The idea got a hold of me and took on a life of it's own.

When an idea gets a hold of you

Wayne Dyer often spoke about inspiration as when an idea gets a hold of you and takes you directly where you were meant to go in the first place and you discover yourself an even greater person you were meant to be. Little did I know, when I arrived in India for my second trip in 2009 and volunteered my time to help write a brochure for my teacher, who provided scholarships to some of the village children, that it would grow into an international charity that I would be involved with, providing free education to underprivileged children in India. This is one example of when an idea got a hold of me – I couldn't have even planned for this. Fast forward eight years later where now I'm an integral part of the organization serving on the board of directors.

Aligning yourself with the source

As mentioned I'm an action-oriented person and I often have challenges giving up control and waiting for the *allowing* part to happen. The allowance is making space for a greater force of creation to enter. This force is beyond our human capabilities. When you align yourself with these positive forces, or the source of creation, you will come to realize that a greater power exists and that you cannot control all of the details in your life. Whether you call it God, or Source, or the Divine, or something else, is up to you. I think of this force as an infinite presence that exists all around me, within nature and within myself.

Now, here's the kicker, as you are visualizing and taking steps towards fulfilling your desires, it's important not to get hung up on exactly *how* or when you will get there. You may have a solid plan, however the forces of creation may have something else in mind for you, there may be other lessons for you to learn on your journey before you fully realize your goals. Sometimes the lessons you need to learn are presented to you in your everyday experience. Be open to possibility and to co-creation with the universe, rather than domination.

Appreciation for what is

Going back to that day when I was traveling in south India sitting in Santana's restaurant, observing what was happening on the beach, I will never forget my conversation with the waiter about the fisherman. I felt an immense appreciation for my life and my family at that moment. It was only a few months before when I was complaining about my job and noticing a lot of negativity around me. Even in moments of darkness of negativity there is always an opportunity to appreciate *something*. Looking back, had I not experienced my previous situation of being overworked and feeling stressed and disconnected from myself I would not have had a place of contrast for the good things in life, such as freedom to travel and time away to reconnect.

As you are working towards your desires with intention, it's easy to get caught up in the end goal, causing you to lose out on the present moment and failing to appreciate what you currently have. This was one of those moments for me. While I was going about my day that day with the intention to read and relax, much of my journal writings around that time were focused on where I would travel to next, how I was going to start up my own yoga classes and what I wanted to do with the rest of my life. It's pretty daunting if you're trying to plan out your whole life in a few weeks! I've since learned that planning every detail of life is not possible, it's so much more fun to go with the flow of life anyway. It's more about holding a vision in mind of what you desire and being open to a variety of ways in which you will arrive or achieve your vision.

Exercise: Set Your Intention with a Vision Board

I mentioned earlier I had created a vision board that was filled with images of beautiful destinations and had a strong theme of travel. I have created a few different vision boards since then. Now is the time for you to take action by creating your vision board. Creating a vision board is a way to put your intentions onto paper and it's an activity you can do alone or with a group of friends.

I gathered a small group of women together at my home for a potluck dinner, for the purpose of creating our vision boards together. We met a few times for more potlucks throughout the year to check in on our progress. It was really interesting to share our successes and funny stories and also to see what had changed since our last meeting. The vision board is meant to serve as an inspiration, to guide you towards what your heart deeply desires.

Whether you are doing this activity solo, or with friends, you will need to gather some supplies such as; old magazines or newspapers, scissors, glue, tape, cardboard or bristol board, markers, stickers and possibly string or glitter – whatever crafts you have on hand.

1. Begin to leaf through the magazines and cut out images and words that resonate with you, things that make you feel happy. Don't worry about what the final vision board will look like at this time – it's a creative process.
2. Once you feel you have enough content, you then begin to layout the images and words on your board. Maybe you want to write a key state-ment or message in the centre – something that you want to bring into

your life? Write this message as if it's already here, not in the future tense.

3. Continue to organize and create your board by gluing or taping the magazine cuttings and adding whatever creative flair you like – there is no wrong way to do this. Take as long as you need until you feel your board is complete.

4. If you're in a group, it's nice to share your board once everyone has finished (if you feel comfortable), maybe talking about the primary theme or why you chose certain images.

5. Place your vision board somewhere prominent, where you will see it every day. Spend a few moments with it each day taking in in visually and observing the feelings that arise.

When you view your vision board, imagine that everything on there is already here and now. Notice if feelings of lack come up when you are looking at your board. For example, my vision board that was filled with images of beautiful beaches and lush jungles, if I was looking at it and feeling that I would never get to visit those places and it was all just a pipe dream, then chances are I would never have gone to places like Fiji and Malaysia and Indonesia, because of my limiting beliefs. However, when I was viewing my board, it was always with feelings of happiness and excitement and an eagerness that visiting these places was just around the corner, even if I had no idea how I would get there or when it would happen. I could imagine myself on the beach, I could smell the salty sea air, and I could feel the humidity of the lush rainforest.

By going through this feeling and vision process daily, you might be surprised at what starts showing up in your life. The items on your board may not manifest exactly the way you have anticipated, nor is the timing fixed. Be open to possibility and trust in the power of your intention.

Chapter Six TRUST YOURSELF: OVERCOME DOUBT

- October 21, 2009 - Here I go again

I should be about half way there at this time. I'm sitting in Brussels airport for the next hour or so before I get on the next flight to Delhi and I'm looking forward to eating delicious Indian food again. I feel like an old pro at this now and it's good to be on the road again. I've racked up thousands of air miles (too bad I haven't actually been collecting them though). I haven't made too many decisions today, other than what to eat, how nice is that? I've lost count of how many places I've visited in the past year. Maybe I'll make a list when I'm on the plane, I'm running out of time - time to board…

- October 23, 2009 – This feels familiar

Good morning: I'm enjoying breakfast on the rooftop at the Smyle Inn - it's my little sanctuary amidst the chaos of Delhi. As I sip my tea I can hear the familiar sounds of the outside world; crazy traffic, honking cars, dogs barking, people chatting, kids playing in the street. It's so vibrant and full of life. I'll venture out after breakfast to take it all in, although I'm treasuring this alone time right now. It may be one of the few times I will be alone over the next few months. Ah, there goes the blaring Bollywood-style music, it makes me smile. I'm so tired after the journey and feeling a little spaced out and my mind is wandering ahead into the future as to what the 500-hour yoga teacher training will bring. I'm not sure how long I'll stay in India this time, my visa lasts six months, so let's see what happens.

Good evening: After a day of running around the city, playing frogger with traffic and going on a wild goose chase to get my train tickets, stupidly booking a trip to Kashmir, then cancelling it, catching up with old friends, and meeting new ones, I'm happily back at the Smyle Inn by myself, feeling tired but unable to sleep. I've had many chances today to test my intuition, to see when I'm really going with the flow or getting taken for a ride being a tourist. I got caught up in the flow of seemingly random events. As I went to the train station to buy my ticket to Rishikesh I was approached outside the station by a young man who asked where I was planning to go and informed me the ticket office was closed. He wanted to know if I would like to go to his travel agency to purchase my ticket there instead. Being open to possibility I said sure! I had purchased a three-day trip to Kashmir to stay on a houseboat thinking that would be a fun diversion before immersing myself in yoga again.

When I got back here this afternoon, something didn't feel right, so I decided to check the travel advisories for the area. While Kashmir is a known area of conflict I didn't realize that violence had flared up in recent days so I went back down to the travel agency and cancelled my plans and managed to get most of my money back. I told Ali, my new friend who works here at Smyle, what happened and he said I had fallen for a scam by being told the train station ticket office was closed and he would help me purchase my ticket to Rishikesh instead. Now I don't know if I can trust him, what if he charges me double the usual price because it's a last minute booking? I'm checking out to-morrow morning to go somewhere, it's now 10:15 pm and I can hear the Hare Krishna bells and donkeys outside my window, it's insanely hot and I'm still feeling restless and not able to sleep – let's see what tomorrow brings.

- October 24, 2009 – Only in Delhi

I'm finally on the train. It's been quite the expedition to get here and it feels like a miracle occurred for me to be sitting in my seat at this time, even though I was up at 5 am and at the station one hour early to grab a bite to eat. Thank God for Ali and for mo-bile phones, is all I can say – he's restored my faith in humanity after the events of yesterday. When I arrived at the station I was looking for train 0411 on the departures board but didn't see it. Someone approached me and told me my train was delayed by nine hours but this didn't seem right, as the train wasn't even listed. I called Ali and he immediately came down to the station to meet me and made it his personal mission to ensure I got on the train and in the right car. Although when I've ended up in the wrong car in the wrong class in the past, I've always had fun. We stared at the departures board together for a few minutes, however that did not make the number appear, then Ali grabbed my backpack and said 'come with me.' We then approached the inquiries counter to see a massive line of what seemed to be hun-dreds of people deep. He shuffled us to the front and we soon dis-covered I was supposed to be at platform 10. Why this wasn't on the departures board I don't know, hari-om as they say in India! We ran to the platform as the train was departing, he got on with me, still carrying my backpack and to make sure I found my seat. As the train was picking up speed we were saying our goodbyes and he jumped off and stood on the platform waving goodbye. It was like something from the movies.

Now I've got about four hours to kill on the train before I arrive in Haridwar and I'm thinking about the craziness of the past few days. I'm glad I didn't let my experiences of yesterday taint my day today. Onwards I go to Rishikesh...

Trust is the opposite of doubt

When Ali offered to help me purchase my train ticket that night back at the guesthouse, after my crazy day, I was initially feeling hesitant due to the detour and mix-up I got involved with earlier in the day. It could have gone either way – I could have been stubborn and insisted that I figure it out on my own and deny his request to help me. Instead I chose to trust that he was genuine and wanted to help me. Thankfully I made the right choice.

Brene Brown, in the *Anatomy of Trust*[1], says that trust is built in the smallest of moments. She explores what it means to trust someone and to trust yourself. She begins by telling the story of her third grade daughter's humiliating experience at school where her daughter had shared a difficult experience with a couple of her friends, who then spilled the story to the rest of the class. This resulted in them laughing and pointing at her and calling her names. For a young girl, this was very traumatic and an early lesson in betrayal of trust. Sometimes that's all it takes, is that one traumatic experience, which could potentially lead to a lifetime of mistrust, if not addressed early on.

I remember an experience when I was eleven, only a few months after arriving in Canada from Ireland. In the local park I discovered that someone had written some nasty graffiti about me calling me all sorts of names in the pavilion next to the baseball diamond. I spent a lot of time in this park climbing in the rafters and I was also on the after school softball team; therefore

---

1   http://www.supersoul.tv/supersoul-sessions/the-anatomy-of-trust

my imagination was running wild about who might have written this.

I felt hurt when I first discovered the graffiti as, to my knowledge, I hadn't made any enemies and I was wondering who could be so mean when they didn't even know me. I was angry and wanted to find out who did it so I could confront them. Sadly I was also wondering if I would be able to fit in. I made an effort to drop my Irish accent and adopt a Canadian accent fairly quickly after that, as I didn't want to be seen as different. While this experience hasn't led to a lifetime of mistrust for me, it did leave a mark, as I'm sensitive to when other people are being bullied and I don't stand for it.

When experiencing a difficult situation around trust, in order to get clarity about the problem, Brene suggests breaking down the issues of trust into smaller parts. When you experience a failure of trust, she recommends it's equally important to examine the situation with the other person as well as ask questions of yourself and describes it with the BRAVING acronym.

Building trust with another

You have small moments when you have the opportunity to build trust and you have the opportunity to betray. Breaking a situation down allows you to evaluate which parts of trust have been broken with another person, to say specifically what's not working and provides the opportunity to work on those parts. When examining a situation with another person, you can ask the following:

Boundaries – does this person respect my boundaries and are they clear about their own boundaries?

Reliability – is this person reliable, do they consistently do what they say they are going to do every time?

Accountability – is this person accountable? When they make a mistake, do they own it, apologize and then make amends?

Vault – will this person protect what I am sharing with them? Do they acknowledge confidentiality? Notice when a person is gossiping about another to you, that the vault may not be sealed when you share your thoughts with them – gossiping is a sure fire way to diminish trust.

Integrity – are they coming from a place of integrity and do they encourage me to do the same? Does the person practice their values instead of just professing them?

Non-judgment – are they judgmental towards me when I share vulnerable parts of myself? Will they still be there for me in non-judgment, and me for them, when one of us is falling apart?

Generosity – can I assume the most generous thing about this person's intentions, words and actions whenever they screw up, and will they return the generous assumption with me? Or do I often assume the worst about another when something goes wrong?

Building trust with yourself

When something hard happens in your life, often you lose trust for yourself by blaming and wondering how you could have been so stupid to allow that event to happen. I certainly went through that thought process with past relationships and with the Kashmir fiasco. When you are reflecting upon a difficult situation, you can ask yourself these questions, using the BRAVING acronym to learn where you need to make changes moving forward. BRAVING with another person builds connection with that person, while BRAVING with you establishes self-love and self-respect, according to Brene.

If you can't count on yourself, you can't ask other people to give you what you don't have. – Brene Brown

In my situation with the train tickets in Delhi, looking at it from the BRAV-ING perspective for me personally:

Boundaries – I didn't honour my own boundaries that day when I took the detour and purchased tickets to Kashmir.

Reliability – I was being unreliable with myself because I ignored my intuition when the young man first approached me at the train station but I went along with him anyway, ignoring the slight uneasy feeling in my belly. I didn't stop to take time to process my feelings in the moment.

Accountability – I did hold myself accountable after the fact. Initially though I blamed the travel agent for encouraging me to go with him.

Vault – This is about being protective of my or another's personal stories. The vault didn't really apply in this particular situation.

Integrity – I didn't stay in my integrity as I went against my better judgment at the time.

Non-judgment – I was definitely judgmental towards myself. I thought I was stupid for getting caught up in events of the day and I continued to judge myself for not listening to my inner voice.

Generosity – I was not generous with myself, however I was generous with the travel agent, as I didn't assume the worst about him. Upon reflection I came to the conclusion that he was just trying to earn a few extra rupees – he saw an opportunity and he took it.

Trust your gut

Knowing when to trust your gut can take practice, especially if you are not used to taking a moment to pause to understand the signals, such as listening to what's going on in your body in the moment. Looking back on the events of that day, had I taken a moment to pause when the travel agent first approached me outside the train station to say that I wanted a moment alone to understand what was happening, I could have saved myself hours of frustration, as well as money. Instead I was caught up in a moment of thinking I was going with the flow - lesson learned. This is a simple example of when I didn't trust myself.

It's in these moments that you build up a bank of trust which helps you navigate the bigger decisions in life, for example, if you are thinking of leaving a marriage, or leaving a career behind to start a new business, moving to another city etc. While other people's opinions do matter and they can help you see different perspectives, relying on too many opinions of others can lead to confusion and too much choice, resulting in stress or anxiety over which path to choose.

> **Reflection:**
> *Can you think of a time when you didn't trust your gut instinct?*

As you reflect, remember that you did your best at the time with the resources you had available. Remind yourself of what that was. Now is the time to start paying attention to your gut so you may choose differently going forward.

What are your signals?

We each have our own unique signals. After much practice, I discovered that when I received a signal for no, whether for a false statement or when experiencing a feeling that something just isn't right, my body feels contracted, my shoulders will slightly hunch forward and I get a hollow feeling or twinge in my belly, like a feeling of being nervous. Whereas when I receive a signal for yes, my body feels lighter, my chest is open and there is no twinge in my belly.

In 2014 I bought my first home based on my 'yes' signals. I had narrowed my search down to a couple of different neighbourhoods in Vancouver. Being a first-time buyer in a hot market could have been quite intimidating, however I had a savvy realtor and my intuition on my side. I knew right away when a place didn't feel right as soon as I walked in as I felt heaviness in my chest and belly. When we viewed the place I now call home, I instantly felt curious when I walked inside and started asking lots of questions. Then it was time to check in with my body to see if this was the right place for me. My realtor, Natalie, sat aside and watched, possibly wondering if I was crazy! I stood facing north in the living room with my feet planted firmly on the floor and silently made a statement to myself 'this is my home.' My body felt light and leaned forward – my signal for 'yes.' As this was a big decision for me, my rational mind wanted to test my intuition further so I repeated this in the bedroom and got the same 'yes' reply. One week later the deal was closed and about a month later I moved in.

The other signal I rely on when something feels really right and I know I'm exactly where I'm meant to be, or I'm feeling in alignment, are goose bumps. Not the goose bumps and shivering from feeling cold, this is a different feeling, my body can be warm, yet at that particular moment, a warm, tingling feeling arrives like a wave that originates in my chest and spreads to my arms and fingertips; sometimes it reaches the back of my neck, or my head. This is my sign that something, energy, beyond me is present and tells me that I'm being supported.

Having faith in something bigger than you

Where are these signals coming from? Is it spirit, the universe, God? Are they all the same? It depends on your beliefs. This is not intended to spark a debate if God exists or if one religious faith is better than another. Live and let live and do no harm, is my mantra when it comes to religion. For me, it comes down to having faith and a belief that omnipresence (of God) exists beyond my physical body. While I was baptised into a Christian faith, I was not raised in a religious household. During my travels I was introduced to different religions, such as Hinduism and Buddhism. I'm still learning about other religions to this day. I also believe that everything is made up of energy and we are all connected to one another, to nature. There is a guiding force present in my life sending me in the direction to experience a life of joy and love.

The challenge of being human is accepting that you may not know it all; you may not have physical, hard evidence of what exists beyond you, yet you continue through life, searching for meaning and purpose, relying on faith and belief that there is a greater plan for you.

Exercise: Connect to Your Gut Instinct

You can practice tuning into your gut instinct right now, wherever you are, as you are reading this book. Once you learn your signals, you will be better able to understand yourself and read your reactions to other people in various situations.

1. If you're not already sitting down, take a moment to make yourself comfortable, sitting up nice and tall with your shoulders slightly drawn back opening your chest. Ensure your feet are firmly planted on the floor if you are sitting in a chair.

2. Take a few slow, deep breaths in and out, to help relax yourself and allow your belly to feel soft.

3. Notice if you feel tension in your body. If you're feeling tightness, take a few more deep breaths, setting the intention that you will become more relaxed with each exhale.

4. Now, out loud, verbally make a *false* statement about yourself that is not emotionally charged. For example, since I'm a woman living in Canada, I would say "I am a man," or "I live in Africa."

5. Notice if you experience any sensations in your body when you make a statement that you know to be false. Experiment with other false statements until you get a sense for what your body's signal for 'no' is. If you don't get a signal the first time you try this exercise, don't worry. Check to see if you are feeling really comfortable physically. Perhaps you can try again lying down.

6. Next, verbally make *true* statements about yourself. For example, I would say "I am a woman," and, "I live in Canada." As you practice, notice any sensations in your body when you make your true

statements. Keep experimenting until you get a sense for what your body's signal for 'yes' is.

7. Starting with simple statements helps to set the foundation so you can recognize your body's signals for 'no', for when a situation or interaction with another person arises in the future doesn't feel right. Some people call this your sixth sense.

As you interact with people, notice how your body responds to different people and situations, the more you practice connecting to your gut and noticing how you feel, the better you will get to know yourself and the messages from your body.

Chapter Seven BREAK THROUGH FEAR

- November 10, 2009 – Scratching the surface

Adjusting to ashram life again. My roommate, Barb, is pretty cool – tattooed and nose-pierced like me and she lives just outside of Ottawa. I wonder if Chetana had a hand in picking roommates again this year? There seems to be a good mix of age ranges on this course. There are many Canadians again and a few more men than my last teacher training, although Matt, from Dublin, handled himself pretty well on the course last year amongst thirty women. The dining hall seems to be more crowded than usual. Perhaps there are many more outside guests coming to eat, we're going to have to eat in shifts, which is motivation to get there on time I suppose to get a seat.

I ran into Meenakshi today in the blue house. As soon as she saw me her eyes lit up and we both had a big grin on our faces. She proudly showed me the business cards that I had ordered about a year before on my last day in Rishikesh after the 200-hour teacher training – I was happy the cards had arrived! We caught up over chai and biscuits and pakoras and she showed me the latest goods in her shop. Her daughter is growing up fast and offered to practice her mendhi skills on me. I'll take her up on it when I find some downtime from the course.

We're a few days into the course and today's theme in class this morning was about getting rid of old samskaras – stories, or impressions left on the mind from past life, childhood and those built up over adulthood. It's those stories we tell ourselves that often aren't true. They are like tracks in the mind, the more we tell them, the more we identify with them and the deeper the grooves become. The good news is we can unravel them and change our story. I'm looking forward to unwrapping more of that, but it's also a little scary at the same time, to find out what's in there, what might be buried.

Perfect timing perhaps, considering the dreams I had last night involving a couple of ex-boyfriends, who were not the best choices. As I was about to become close to them again I came to my senses and took off running. Maybe it's a sign that I'm aware not to repeat the same mistakes in a new relationship or maybe I'm running away from my own stories? Time will tell and I'm sure I will find out what I need to know during this course. Already the physical symptoms of detox; headaches and an excited belly, are showing up as I'm adapting again to much more yoga and a healthier diet.

Coming back to samskaras, we learned that we can become attached to our stories because we think they define who we are and because we think they are serving our purpose, whereas if we were able to shed them, we would see our true nature that we came into this earth with, as Vishva says 'joyful, playful, fearless, expandable.' When we are happy and playful we are being our true selves. I was my true self, enjoying Bollywood dancing earlier - that was fun! We also explored more about when we hang onto our own stories unconsciously, that this limits our growth or we could be avoiding something we don't want to deal with. I wonder what aspects of my own growth I'm avoiding? This is the perfect place to find out.

Something that just came to mind is my identity – why do I always have a difficult time giving a straight answer when people ask me where I'm from, a question I get asked a lot while traveling. Based on recent places I've lived I could say London or Toronto, but then I feel compelled to say I'm originally from Ireland. Where is home? Is it based on how much time you've spent in a place or where your family is? Or is it based on where you are right now and where you feel good? Do I identify with being Canadian or am I Irish, then the question goes further, Northern Ireland or the South, which in my mind, Ireland is Ireland and forget The Troubles that have split up the country in the past – at least things are much better now. Do people even care where I'm from or am I just making too much out of this? When I say I'm originally from Ireland, it's usually met with the response that I don't have my accent. Does an accent define me? It's really interesting to start to peel away these layers. Maybe I'll work on coming up with a simple answer to the question of where I'm from for the next person who asks.

I've been planning my first one-on-one yoga class and the theme is on the heart chakra. One thing the heart chakra is related to is the fear of intimacy or fear of relationships or openness to relationships. I want to focus on the openness and healing parts, incorporating breath-work with the arms, representing reaching out and taking in. The heart chakra is represented by a green six-pointed star. It's like two triangles intersecting with the downward movement of spirit into matter and the upward movement of matter into spirit. The goal, if there even should be a goal, is integrating mind, body and spirit and with balance this implies an internal balance with various aspects of ourselves. To balance the conscious/unconscious or

85

*personal and shadow selves, as well as balance with ourselves
and the world around us. Alarm is set for 4:55 am, time to go to
sleep.*

- November 13, 2009 – Digging deeper

*Coming back again to my stories, I'm relaxing and writing
with tea and digestive biscuits, I suppose that's better than
chocolate and ice cream. See how easy it is for me to distract
myself? There I go again indulging in food fantasies – my stories, what are they? Today in class we talked about our personalities and sub-personalities, those little voices in our head that
feed us information and what we think defines us. There were
quite a few tears shed in the group, I almost shed some tears
of empathy, but I held back. Perhaps a fear of looking weak or
being vulnerable – why is that? I discovered that Little Miss
Achiever is one of my sub-personalities. I was reminded about
the story I wrote last year about The Quest for the Firebird,
when I am always looking ahead to the next accomplishment,
that I risk missing out on the very thing that I need that is right
in front of me in this moment. I still struggle with this but at
least it's in my awareness now so I can catch myself before I go
too far off the rails. I'd like to stop story-telling and imagining
the future so much because the story will unfold as it's meant
to and in good time, I'd like to be more present but I seem to get
impatient.*

*One thing I've learned this week is to be a witness, a witness
to my thoughts, to my surroundings and a witness to the present moment to see what's being stirred in my body emotionally
when I encounter various people and situations. Witnessing
this very moment as I re-read what I've just written, it comes*

down to fear – fear of not being enough as I am, needing to be surrounded by accomplishments. I often joke that because I'm the first-born and an Aries that I like to be number one. I do like to go first but the energy underneath the achieving part is what I need to look at. Is it coming from a place of taking action because I enjoy it or because I'm trying to fill a void or fear of not being enough? Something to ponder further... this shit is getting real; I can no longer hide or bury what needs to come out.

Fear and love

On my last day in Rishikesh in 2008 when I was saying goodbye to Vishva, I said, 'I will be back.' He giggled and said 'hari-om'. I knew at that time I would come back to India but I didn't know then that it would be for my second yoga teacher training. In 2009 it was time to go deeper into self-awareness. I had only scratched the surface the previous year and I was curious to uncover more about myself.

I had created my dream life in the previous year; I was traveling around the world, making money and teaching yoga yet I felt there was still some dust to clear in my heart. The heart chakra, feeling joy, love and compassion sounded good in theory but I wasn't fully feeling it and living it every day to the extent that I believed was possible. I was craving a deep and meaningful connection with a man. I desired to be more honest and to create a deeper connection with myself; by allowing myself to be more vulnerable with other people. But there was still fear holding me back then.

I was beginning to question my identity further and when I started to examine my labels I wondered what would be left if I wasn't defined by these things. For example, I am Irish, I am Canadian, I am a daughter, I am a sister, I am a friend, I am a lover, I am a yoga teacher. One of the first exercises we did in pairs on the 500-hour training in the ashram was to sit on the floor across from our partner (who was a total stranger at that time) and answer the question 'Who are you?'

The first person would repeat only those three words while the second person answered. The first person was to keep asking the question, while not offering any other responses or judgment as to the answers the second person was giving. I remember sitting across from my partner Herb, a lovely man in his sixties who had kind eyes and a gentle smile. He kept asking me 'Who Are You?' I started with who I was at work, 'I'm a manager,' because it was an easy place to go. I then elaborated with my relationships to others, 'I'm a sister,' 'I'm a friend,' etc. Then I got uncomfortable as I felt I was running out of answers – *why does he keep asking me'* I wondered?

It was all part of the exercise, to encourage us to go deeper. I felt more awkward as I was getting stuck and with a nervous laugh and feeling the heat in my cheeks I eventually said 'I don't know.' Thankfully my part of the exercise was over and it was my turn to ask Herb who he was!

Reflection:
What are some labels that you identify with? You may also want to try the above exercise of 'Who are you' with a friend or partner.

At the end of the exercise Vishva shared with us that ultimately we are love. That's one thing I didn't say during the exercise. In yogic philosophy the concept of "I am that," which is spoken in the mantra 'So Hum,' means you are identifying yourself with universe or ultimate reality – there is no separation between you and another or in nature. I thought it was a far out concept when I first heard it but now it makes more sense as I've had time to ponder the idea, meditate on it and experience it.

Your false identity

Fear around releasing your labels or identity is something that's very common in the coaching work that I do with others. Even if you are holding on to an identity that is not serving you, it can be scary to think of what might happen or who you will be when you let that go. The identity often acts as a security blanket, allowing you to feel protected because it's been built up over time and it's all you know. Once people find the strength and support to release the blanket, they feel lighter and often wonder why they held onto it for so long.

Struggling with vulnerability

During our teacher training, many people stepped up and shared their deepest feelings, fears and insecurities. I was holding back and was struggling with vulnerability at that time, which now I recognize goes deeper than the over-achieving habits and has roots of fear of being seen and fear of judgment – something that I've learned, by starting to open up, is shared by many people. As my peers on the course were sharing deeply personal experiences, shedding tears and opening up, I was hiding underneath my blanket of fear of being judged for being weak by crying in public, therefore I was holding back in the group exercises.

I've heard many times that love and fear cannot exist in the same moment and I've experienced this to be true. When I'm coming from a place of fear or worry of being seen for who I really am, I'm not loving myself. Now that I know more, nothing disastrous has happened during the times when I've consciously thought to screw fear and be myself anyway. There are still moments when I hold back from fully expressing myself due to some fear that I've created in my head, however for those moments when I do share what I'm really feeling and speaking my truth, risking feeling stupid or embarrassed, nothing bad has happened and I feel relief afterwards. At the end of the 'Who Are You' exercise I was relieved to find out I wasn't the only person who was feeling awkward and struggling to come up with answers.

Real versus perceived fear

There is logical fear, that keeps you safe when you are in danger, where the body automatically kicks in to elicit the fight or flight or freeze reaction, to respond to real danger. The body is an amazing thing, taking care of your primal safety needs so you don't even have to think about it. When there is immediate and obvious danger that threatens your survival, your body is flooded with chemicals like adrenaline and cortisol, which further increases your respiratory rate, and then directs blood away from your vital organs into your muscles and limbs, preparing you to run or fight.

Your awareness of your surroundings also intensifies, your impulses become sharper and your pupils dilate as you move into 'attack' mode.

While your body's reaction to a real threat is useful if you're faced with a tiger in the jungle, or being held at gunpoint, your body doesn't always understand the difference of real threat and a perceived or mind-induced fear. Early in the 500-hour yoga teacher training, when it was my turn to share my personal experiences in group exercises, my mind-induced fear of being seen caused my heart to pound, my body temperature to rise, and I experienced the nervous feeling of butterflies in my stomach. Although sometimes it felt like there was a herd of elephants in there!

I knew the fear wasn't around public speaking because I generally didn't feel afraid in front of a group when I was teaching – it was when all eyes were on me to share more about me (the real me), was when the fear kicked in. The more I practiced sharing and being vulnerable, the more I realized that being seen really wasn't life threatening. During the course of the six weeks training, the physical symptoms of feeling nervous while sharing in the group eventually did subside.

How else does fear show up for you?

Other representations of emotions of fear are jealousy, anger, resentment, and cravings – essentially any time you experience a loss of power or control. More subtle representations of fear are judgment, analyzing, comparing, and planning your response instead of listening to another while being present.[1] I experienced many of these representations of fear, especially during my time in India when I was required to be vulnerable. I still experience some of them today, such as judgment of myself and others, over-analyzing situations and planning responses. I'm usually able to catch myself in the moment and stop these behaviours, but not always.

It's important to understand when it's necessary to allow yourself to experience your emotions fully to ride them out, to release them, versus pasting a fake smile on your face and to stuff the emotions away. When emotions are not fully addressed, they will return until you learn to transform them. I'm not suggesting you ignore the representations of fear, but rather *recognize* when they occur so you can step back or take the necessary alone time to process them without taking them out on another person. Taking time out to be alone can be challenging in today's busy world.

The busyness culture

One of the challenges in today's society and culture of busyness is that when you are constantly running around at top speed, taking little time to slow down, the mind is overworked and small fears and anxieties can easily balloon into major problems if you don't pause once in a while. This is when repetitive thoughts occur where you imagine the worst possible outcome. When you are continuously immersed in stressful situations, your body becomes flooded with stress hormones, shallow breathing occurs, the heart starts beating faster, body temperature will fluctuate and the body can even-

---

1   Gary Zukav: Spiritual Partnership, p 147.

tually spiral into a state of panic.

Practice awareness

With practice, you have the ability to cultivate a deep and even flow of breath, sending it deeper into the belly, which promotes a healthy exchange of gases and sends a signal to the body to relax. This allows you to ward off a potential state of panic before it balloons out of control. If you feel your breath is shallow, pause and take a slow, deep inhalation, then an equal or longer exhalation. Just a few cycles of this can instantly change your mood and break the negative feedback loop from the mind to body when there is no real danger or threat to our survival.

> **Reflection:**
> *Pause and take three, long slow breaths right now. Imagine you are sending your breath deep into your belly with your inhale. Notice your belly fall with your exhale.*

How do you feel after slowing down your breathing? It's in the small moments by ourselves or in relationship with another person, where you can choose to examine your reactions, your thoughts and pattern of breath, to make a commitment to react to a situation with love or fear, making tiny changes one step at a time. Once you become more aware of your re-actions in real-time, you will realize you are in complete control over the creation of your reality and you can choose to react from a place of love, instead of fear, whenever you feel fearful emotions. It starts with making a personal commitment to choose love over fear, in each moment, or when a challenge is presented and by making it a priority to learn more about yourself each time.

Developing emotional awareness takes practice, and it's not something that you master completely. It's a continuous learning process. When you catch yourself in these moments, in addition to the deeper breathing, begin to tune into your body to feel what's going on by acknowledging what kind of emotion you are experiencing.

To tune into your body, as you are breathing in, notice where in your body you feel a restriction or tightness. On the inhalation, imagine you are expanding that area of your body with your breath and on the exhalation, imagine yourself letting go of the emotion. If you need to take it one step further, you could try to imagine yourself observing your reaction, as if you were watching a dear friend or a loved one, and envision what you might say to that person or how you might offer support to help them through this difficult period.

By slowing down the breath, being present and tuning into the body, you challenge the fearful reactions or experiences of the mind, which allows you to rein in the fear (by not letting your negative emotions run wild and control you). This helps to transform your reactions by cultivating an opposite, more positive response.

What are your beliefs?

Fear and doubt are often rooted in your beliefs, which are formed at a very young age, and continue to be formed throughout your life, based on your life experiences. They can become a self-fulfilling prophecy, which is great if they are positive and are leading you down the right path for personal growth. When beliefs are negative or false, you take yourself down a more challenging or painful path of growth. There are various ways to journey through life and many possible paths to venture down. The question to ponder is: how easy and enjoyable do you wish to make this journey?

Exercise: Examine Your Beliefs

How often have you stopped to question your beliefs to examine if they are really true? By examining your beliefs and challenging them, you have the ability to change them, therefore producing different results based on your expectations.

Get out your journal and find a time and place where you can focus. Try to complete the exercise in its entirety. If it feels overwhelming, complete Step 1 and focus on ONE section of beliefs, before proceeding to step 9 and 10 (review and evaluation).[2]

Step 1: Write down ten significant **traumatic** and ten **empowering** events from your childhood. Write as quickly as you can without pausing to analyze your responses.

Step 2: Write down your beliefs about work (try to fill the page).

Here are some examples to guide you:

- Work should be fulfilling as we spend a lot of time doing it.
- Work is my way of contributing to the world.
- Work is stressful. Stress is needed in order to get ahead. (Limiting belief)
- I believe that my coworkers like me.
- I like that work is close to my home, reducing commute time as my

---

2   Beliefs exercise taken from Coaching Horizons course manual, Become a Body Mind Spirit Coach, Barb Pierce.

time is important.

Step 3: Write down your beliefs about sex (try to fill the page). Write as quickly as you can without pausing to analyze.

Step 4: Write down your beliefs about family (try to fill the page). Write as quickly as you can without pausing to analyze.

Step 5: Write down your beliefs about friends (try to fill the page). Write as quickly as you can without pausing to analyze.

Step 6: Write down your beliefs about friends (try to fill the page). Write as quickly as you can without pausing to analyze.

Step 7: Write down any other beliefs about life that you have. These are beliefs that are not covered in any of the categories above.

Step 8: Try and write even more of your beliefs — beyond the obvious, everyday ones — to the ones that may not be top of mind but that drive your behaviours in subtle ways.

Step 9: Review, evaluate and reset.
When you feel that you are done, go back and review your lists. For each area, identify which beliefs are true and which beliefs are 'limiting beliefs'— beliefs that are artificially holding you back from fully living your life. This portion of the exercise helps you to reconsider these limiting beliefs and of-

fers you ways to begin changing the way you think about these areas of your life.

Limiting belief:

Work is stressful. Stress is needed in order to get ahead.

How my limiting belief has affected me:

I have become stressed at work by taking on too much in order to prove myself and have allowed it to interfere in my personal life and health by feeling grumpy, tired, and frustrated.

New belief:

Work does not need to be stressful.

List any new skills or resources required to make this belief change:

I will notice when I'm feeling stressed or frustrated and will challenge my thought pattern. There will be help available and a solution is possible if I ask for help. When I ask for help, I can solve problems sooner and I do not take the stress home with me, nor allow it to interfere with my personal life or health.

Continue going through the exercises for each limiting belief you have identified and write out your new belief, and then identify any resources or skills to make this belief change.

Step 10: Reflection.

Did you notice any patterns or receive insights from your childhood traumatic and empowering experiences that have had an impact on your beliefs now? What beliefs do you have that may not be 100% true? How would your life be better if you were living it based on the new empowering beliefs?

Chapter Eight Gratitude

- November 17, 2009 – Discovering my true being

By 6 p.m. last night I was ready for bed, due to my lack of sleep the previous night. I managed to stay awake reading until 7:30 pm, then I crashed and had a wonderful sleep - probably why I feel so good today. It rained quite heavily at the end of our morning meditation and it felt amazing. My body was comfortable, it was warm, cool and tingling at the same time and I had a silly grin on my face as I was meditating on connecting with my heart centre.

The theme today is practicing being with yourself - the more you practice this the more you discover and are comfortable with your true being, which is one of happiness and simplicity. Well I haven't yet broken down into any tears or had any shocking revelations, so maybe happiness and simplicity is just around the corner, or maybe it's already here and available for me.

I'm wondering if there is something lurking underneath and between my moments of bliss and the pain is on it's way to the surface, but maybe not. In the meantime, why not enjoy the good feelings I'm having. Maybe I am truly happy with myself and yes it feels great, my silly grin is coming back. This doesn't mean I won't experience sadness, frustration, anger, or those kinds of emotions in the future, however I'm choosing right now to enjoy my day and I believe that in the end, all will be well. I love the smell of the air after the rain.

I meditated on my right hip this morning, as it's been feeling sore lately and after meditation it felt a little better. This mind-body medicine really has something to do with it. I've been having a pain in my right hip for a few years now. It doesn't bother me when I'm running but sometimes a throbbing pain just surfaces, deep in the piriformis muscle. I think the pain in my hip could be related to my time in Vancouver as that's when I recall it first started. Maybe it's related to my relationship to Adam but I'm not sure. It's time to put the pain in my hip behind me and to heal my heart. The heart might take a little longer to heal but that's okay, it will happen.

- November 22, 2009 – Digging deeper

I began my silence last night and shortly before going to bed I had the most intense massage with incredibly hot herbs placed on my hip. After the massage I had a good cry, not total floodgates type of cry, and I wasn't even sure why I was crying but it came out nonetheless. I'll probably have some bruises tomorrow. The more I meditate on this, the more I'm convinced that I've found the root of my problem and now it's time to heal - it's amazing what the mind and body can accomplish when it wants to. My mind is all over the place, what ramblings, over the last few days a negative thought, then a positive one, then a negative one, then a positive one, this is exhausting.

- November 25, 2009 – Shaken to the core

I had an insane experience in my body last night and I can't even bring myself to fully describe it right now as I'm still digesting what happened. I feel so much lighter and I believe my stomach troubles and the pain in my hip will disappear very soon. Swami Yogananda-ji, the 100-year-old Yogi came to teach our class this morning. He was ready and excited at 2 a.m. and walked for two hours to get here. It's impossible to feel weak when you are in the presence of this man -he can put both of his legs behind his head while showing off his battle scars from being a freedom fighter when he was younger. He has ten children and I believe only three remain alive. His secret is laughing lots, eating fruit, honey and rice and he even proved to us that his teeth are still intact – priceless! What an inspiration.

- December 11, 2009 – The end and a new beginning

It's the final day of our 500-hour training and I've experienced a wide range of emotions in the past couple of days. Last night at kirtan I was feeling mostly happy and then Radha sang a beautiful song in English (Door of my heart) and I became quite emotional. Finally I shed some tears in public - I was crying because the course is coming to an end and I was thinking this was the last time we would all be together. I hate endings, I suck at goodbyes. I always get worked up before it's time to say goodbye to someone then after we go our separate ways, I am fine. I was crying for a part of myself, saying goodbye to old pain, it was kind of a relief.

This is an ending, but it's also a new beginning and the next part of my adventure begins now. The ending and shedding of stuff I don't need and the beginning of something new, redefining myself. Last night in my dreams, the only thing I really remember was I trying to choose a book from a bookshelf and all of them had 'light' in the title and I wasn't sure which one to pick. I took each one of the books off the shelf and leafed through them, then put them back and sat there contemplating my options. I eventually chose the book that had dancing and light in the title. I can interpret this however I wish. I believe there are many ways I can shine my light and the point is to just pick something and go for it, there are many other books on the shelf to choose from, or many paths to enlightenment as they say.

Visvha is an incredible teacher and I am so happy and proud to have studied with him. I intend to share my knowledge and my love through my teaching, to really love from the heart. Its no longer necessary to be a stone with my emotions. I felt a beautiful and warm sensation in my chest today during savasana, perhaps that's a sign that I am truly opening and I have a feeling that something is just around the corner, yet I'm to remain present and continue to surrender to now in order to fully experience life. It would be interesting to read my journal from this time last year to see how things have changed and how I have changed - I definitely feel more at peace – thank you India!

Oh and I volunteered to help Vishva today by writing a brochure to help get sponsors for the kids he's supporting in the village. There are a few children in and around the ashram and he provides scholarships for them to go to school to help cover costs of books and uniforms.

Change your mindset with gratitude

During the last weeks of the yoga teacher training, my mind and body was fully put to the test. We were practicing yoga and meditation sometimes up to five or six hours a day. Adding on the study time and philosophy classes, we typically experienced a twelve-hour day, six days a week.

In 2008 when I completed my first teacher training I thought I had life all figured out, yet I realized one year later that there was still more personal work to be done to clear old pain from past relationships. In yogic philosophy one of the concepts we learned was that yoga is about reducing the cessation of thought waves in the mind. Towards the end of the training I had a full storm in my mind. However it began to pass the more I leaned into and faced my fears of being vulnerable around others and the more I had compassion for myself for allowing myself to get into an unhealthy relationship with Adam. I believe I was storing my emotional pain in my right hip for many years and it took a lot of introspection during my time in India to connect the dots to finally release the pain, both physically and emotionally. Even though these were difficult times I look back now and appreciate what I went through. I have gratitude that I was able to come out on the other side a stronger person as a result.

Reflection:
Think of a difficult time in your life. Was there a lesson learned or have you gained something positive because of that experience?

Notice how you are feeling now after your reflection upon a difficult time in your life. Remember, fear and anger cannot exist at the same time as gratitude. Practicing gratitude allows you to turn your mindset around in a second. When you are appreciating something in your life, or feeling grateful, try being angry or fearful at the same time – it doesn't work. No matter what is going on in your life, chances are there is something in this moment that you can be grateful for. Even if your world is turned upside down, there

101

may be a blessing in disguise that will be revealed as a result of you having gone through the difficult situation, even if you cannot see it at the time.

This is not about pushing aside or ignoring your emotions. Instead of running a particular story of anger or despair or sadness, beyond where it needs to go, I encourage you to look for the smallest things that you are grateful for. This shifts your perspective and changes the energy around you and the situation. Practicing gratitude can diminish the negative effects on your soul.

The obvious things I'm grateful for are my family and friends, to have a roof over my head and food in the fridge, my basic needs are taken care of. I'm also grateful for my resourcefulness and my ability to be open to possibility, as this has allowed me to take my career on the road, to work and to travel to places where I've met so many amazing people and learned just how fortunate I am. Traveling in developing countries has validated my thoughts that people don't need to be surrounded by luxury in order to be happy.

I'm grateful for the kindness of strangers. I've lost count over the amount of times on my travels that I've been welcomed into a family's home for a meal when they have just met me and they ask for nothing in return. I remember a few years ago when I was traveling in Morocco with my best friend Louise, we met a family on the train traveling from Tangier to Fez and struck up a conversation with a local teacher. He asked us where we were going and where we were staying. Being true backpackers we had no plan of where to stay until we arrived at our destination and had a chance to look around. He was traveling with a mother and her two children and the kids were in his class. When she graciously offered for us to stay with them we happily accepted. We found out when we arrived we would be sharing the couch in the living room with the kids and that was ok with us. The family lived in a modest apartment and we enjoyed three days with them, immersing ourselves in their lives, practicing French and Arabic, and sharing family meals. They showed us around town and they asked for nothing in return.

We insisted that we contribute to the grocery bill for the meals. It's easy to find gratitude when things are going well, the challenging part is finding something to be grateful for during hard times.

Finding gratitude in difficult times

I know that you have experienced some difficult times in your life; while the degree of tragedy will vary, nobody is immune to life's challenges. I consider myself fortunate as I have my health, a good family and supportive friends. While I have gone through difficult times, I have not experienced tragedy of great magnitude. My dear friend Ryan, who I've known for over twenty years, continues to be an inspiration to me. His life was changed drastically in a moment on February 17th, 2004 when he had a tragic accident at work where he was crushed by a car and almost died. He has been through so much and lives in constant pain, yet not once have I heard him complain. He serves as a reminder to me to appreciate each day for the gift that it is and to find pleasure in the simple things.

Exercise: Practice Gratitude

I suggest creating a daily ritual to acknowledge things in your life that you are thankful for. Whether you are thinking about things to be grateful for or writing a list each day, this should only take up a few minutes of your time. If you are stuck on what to be grateful for, start with simple things, such as the smell of the ocean, the warm sun on your face, your child's smile. Once you start finding things you are grateful for, you will be able to get more specific and your list will grow.

Following are some ways to practice gratitude – try them out to see what resonates, or create your own way:

1. Find a visual representation of something or someone whom you are grateful for and place this in a spot where you will see it every day, for example on your bedside table or your fridge. When you see this image or word, pause for a moment to take it in and enjoy the positive feelings in your body that this image generates.
2. Keep a gratitude journal. Each morning, or before you go to bed at night, take a few minutes to write in your journal, three things that you are grateful for. After practicing this for a while, you may even wish to expand the list beyond three.
3. Call up an old friend or family member, someone whom you haven't spoken to in a while and tell her something about her that you appreciate. It may surprise you how much of an impact this can have on a person.
4. Take the previous suggestion one step further and make a list of the important people in your life. When was the last time you complimented them or shared why you value their presence? Make a date to call, email or text each person on your list, to say something nice

and to let him or her know you are thinking of them and you are grateful to have them in your life.

5. Going even further, think of a difficult person in your life and reflect on a particular situation in which you may have been upset or angry with this person. Now that you can examine the bigger picture, ask yourself, what lesson did this person help teach you about yourself? Can you find gratitude from a difficult interaction? It's up to you whether or not you wish to reach out to this person to say thank you.

6. Last but not least, appreciate and have gratitude for yourself. You often are hardest on yourself and the most challenging task could be to appreciate your own qualities. You may wish to journal about this. If you're having trouble getting started, think of a time when you did something really well, or were praised by another person. What qualities did you exhibit that this person thought were great? Think of a time when you felt joy or happiness. What was it about that situation that you contributed to? Focusing on and appreciating your strengths, rather than focusing on what you think you're not good at, helps you to cultivate more of the positive traits and behaviour into your life.

Chapter Nine Joy

- December, 13, 2009 – Life in Rishikesh

Puppy duty started this morning, they are so adorable. Today I officially take over from Meera as she is heading home. I've given them good Irish names: Una, Finula, Amanda and Sioban. Mama bear or Kali, their mother, came by to feed them just as I was leaving to head out for the day.

Meera, one of the teachers on our 500-hour course, found the puppies behind the ashram in the bushes. We think the mother Kali might have rabies. A few of us have taken it upon ourselves to provide them with food and shelter and we're trying to get the vet to come out to give them shots. There's not a lot of respect for dogs here, most of them have to fend for themselves, although some people do have pets in their homes, it's not common – the cows are more revered. I've also been warned about petting the dogs in case I get bitten and will need rabies shots, but I'll take my chances.

The course has ended and I'm settling into life in Rishikesh as I'll be here over the winter, or maybe longer. I have the opportunity to teach regularly at the ashram, which is amazing. I've signed up to volunteer at Ramana's garden –the orphanage where I'll be helping out with after school tuition, mostly with the kids aged 6 and under, it should be fun. Otherwise I've been hanging out with some of the other ashram regulars and getting used to a more relaxed pace after the course. This is my time to integrate the teachings and to enjoy my surroundings.

- December 14, 2009 – The flood

Last night the puppies were flooded out of their makeshift home and thankfully the building security guard of the construction site next door rescued them and has taken them in. I went to check on them and was flagged down by the building manager (I think I'm known as the dog lady now) and he took me to the construction site manager's house, where the puppies were huddled together at the front door. They had received the royal treatment of being washed and blow-dried and were given fresh milk and treats. We had coffee and a chat about what to do with the puppies, as it was confirmed that their mother, Kali, is sick and dying of rabies. For now they will remain at the construction site and we'll keep checking on them daily to bring them food.

I started at Ramana's Garden today. The lead volunteer wasn't there to show me around so I figured out things on my own. The kids are really cute. We spent the day in the garden and they showed me the roof where they often study. We spent a little time on homework and a lot more time playing, as they were more interested in chasing dogs and pointing out monkeys than copying out their words from Hindi to English – who can blame them?

Two of the girls seemed to take a shine to me, Preethi and Pinky. Within a minute of meeting Preethi, she said, "I love you," which was sweet and struck me at the same time. I also learned that the kids do yoga everyday, I would have loved to have learned yoga in primary school. We're doing arts and crafts tomorrow and they have some special activities planned at Christmas that they would like my help with, I think I'm really going to like this place.

- December 16, 2009 – Settling into routine

The dogs have been renamed Jenny, Jerry, Jackie and Julie by the construction manager's kids! I guess the Irish names didn't stick. Since I'm staying here for a while I've decided to take Hindi lessons, so I can better communicate with people in the villages. I'm getting used to this slower pace of life and I like my daily routine. Each day I have a few responsibilities such as teaching yoga, volunteering at Ramana's and playing with the puppies, everything else just seems to fall into place with no plans - I love going with the flow. I'm thinking of taking drumming and singing lessons, exploring painting and of course it's great to have time to write every day.

I'm at the German Bakery, waiting for my masala chai to arrive – my new daily ritual and small caffeine fix, which keeps me alert for all the people watching as the tourists and locals and dogs and monkeys and cows and motorbikes weave their way across Laxman Jhula bridge. It's organized chaos, it all seems to work, just like the traffic in Delhi. The monkeys are cute and also a bit scary and they will stop at nothing to steal the tourist's food – it's funny to watch. As I'm here most days the staff know me now and I rarely have to order, as they seem to know I will be ordering chai. I'm a creature of habit!

It's a beautiful morning as I sit here, mesmerized by the mountains. I'm feeling Santosha (contentment).

- December 25, 2009 - Merry Christmas

I woke up to go to class this morning to find a little surprise – my door had been decorated with ribbon. When I returned from class, there was a small gift waiting for me. It was an orange and a candy cane, as well as a little note inviting me to join in a special celebration at breakfast with apple cider. It's the simple things that bring happiness; nobody needs piles of presents on Christmas morning. Still, I remember it was exciting as a kid, tiptoeing into the room in the morning in case Santa was still putting out presents, then to find our pile of presents under the tree.

Our blanket fund is growing and we're going to the market to-day to buy some to hand out, along with children's clothes. Then we're off to Ramana's Garden to sing songs with the children and then it's dinner at Tulsi restaurant. I think there's around twenty of us going now; we've formed a great little community here. Even though I miss my family and I'm thinking of them, to me, this is the real meaning of Christmas – appreciating the small things, giving what you can, opening your heart and sharing with your loved ones - I am so filled with joy.

I finished the brochure that describes Vishva's program for supporting the local kids to go to school. Maybe I could build a website for this? I've been in touch with some of the other yoga teachers on the 500-hour course and there is talk about making this official so we can help more people. Let's keep this idea brewing...

Finding joy in simple pleasures

Looking back over my journal after the course and when I was settling into daily life in the ashram, I realize I truly was content and was experiencing joy easily each day. Even though family and good friends, who have known me for a long time, weren't with me, I was surrounded by a new group of friends and had a real sense of community within the ashram and in the surrounding village.

It was easy to find joy in the ashram environment as all of our basic needs for food and accommodation were taken care of, along with a daily spiritual practice. We didn't have to worry about life's daily stresses; instead I spent my days with no particular agenda, other than my teaching schedule and my time volunteering at the orphanage. I tended to go with the flow and always managed to bump into the right people at the right time to enjoy the day with. The key for me was to cultivate this sense of spontaneity and joyfulness outside of the ashram, once the pressures of the faster-paced, Western lifestyle were presented again upon my return to Canada – a lifestyle that I previously created where I was tied to a schedule at work and often had to schedule in social time with friends.

Spending time with the puppies and the kids at the orphanage helped me realize that as the older I've got, I've noticed the less playful I've become. It was too easy for me to get caught up in the humdrum of daily life and I needed to make a conscious effort to play more, to be silly every day, to laugh. I had to retrain myself to experience joy to the point where it's become a dominant part of my nature again.

Reflection:
Take a moment to think about your week ahead. What feelings arise when you are envisioning how you will spend your week? Are you looking ahead with excitement? What fun activities will you do?

It's all about perception

I've since learned that it's my perception of my experiences that matters. If I perceive my life to be full of pressure and one that requires constant scheduling, then it will be so. If I perceive it as the opposite, and keep activating the happier feelings of going with the flow, as I did in India, then *that* will be my experience. I have the power to change my perception and circumstances any time I'm not feeling happy with what I'm doing. Joy may arrive spontaneously and it's also something that can be cultivated through practice. It's helpful to have a reminder from the wise words of my teacher.

 You are joyful, playful, fearless, expandable. – Yogrishi Vishvketu

Exercise: Create Your Joy List

If you've been feeling that your life has been lacking in playfulness or joy lately, I encourage you to focus on the things that make you happy and make a commitment to yourself to set aside time to do them – create your joy list.

1. Get out your journal and start writing a list of things that bring you happiness or joy, whether it's a fun activity or sport, or spending time with a particular person.

2. Come up with at least ten items. Then challenge yourself to come up with at least three more.

3. Review your list and put a date beside the last time you participated in each activity. If you can't remember, put a big question mark beside that item.

4. Now, take a closer look at your list. Is there anything on there that you could do right away or participate in more than once during the week? Maybe a small pleasure that doesn't cost anything, nor take up a lot of your time. If so then make a commitment to do this one thing today. There's no time like the present.

5. Keep going through your list and place a date beside each item on your list for when you will do that activity. Be realistic with your time, there's no need to schedule them all within the next week. If you're ultra organized, schedule time in your calendar and set a reminder so these activities take priority, along with the other obligations in your life.

6. Revisit this list from time to time and acknowledge when you are do-ing something fun for yourself. If, after a few weeks, you've noticed

you've slipped into old habits and are no longer checking your joy list, then either recommit to yourself to start it up again, or find a support buddy. Creating this list with a friend is a great way to keep the momentum going by encouraging each other and holding one another accountable for having fun.

Chapter Ten

- December 31, 2009 – The end of another year

I woke up this morning and decided to do my own practice, which included a few sun salutations and a meditation, followed by cleaning out my nose with the neti pot. My shoulders and hips are feeling a bit more relaxed today, I think I overdid it in class the past few days.

I've been reading my first Jiddu Krishnamurti book about fear. It's interesting, because I remember Barb's comment on anxiety about it really being a state of mind that exists around thoughts of the future, which neither really exist, since all we truly have is the present moment. So is it possible to feel anxious if we bring ourselves completely into the present moment?

What are my fears? Perhaps that I will be alone, but then we are all alone. While a lot of my friends are married with kids now, Krishnamurti also talks about comparison and that by comparing ourselves to others essentially breeds fear – it's true. If I stop and witness at this very moment, I'm not afraid of anything. The future is full of possibility, we're on the cusp of a blue moon and it is shining bright and beautiful tonight. I will set my alarm later as we are welcoming in the New Year by chanting the Gayatri Mantra. It's the first time we will all be awake at midnight at the ashram as we're normally in bed by 9 pm.

Now here I am avoiding writing about fear by jumping ahead to tonight. What else do I fear? Now that the Little Miss Achiever part of my personality has been exposed, and the fear of not being accepted or fear of not being enough, has come to light, there really isn't much else to fear. Screw fear! I choose happiness. What a freeing feeling. What a fantastic year I've had, I'm looking forward to what's possible in 2010, starting with a New Year's Day dip in the Ganga, and it's going to be chilly but fun.

May you may feel protected and safe,
May you feel contented and pleased,
May your body support you with strength,
May your life unfold smoothly and with ease.

- January 2, 2010 – Happy New Year!

It certainly was freezing but absolutely refreshing and a lot of fun. We sprinted like crazy people into the Ganga yesterday, then gathered in a circle and held hands while we dipped under a few times together, bringing in good wishes for the new year ahead. After drying off we ventured off to the other side of the bridge to the Freedom Café for chai. We had quite the crew; Archna, Julia, Christie, Anand, Ravi, Gaurav, Pook and I spent most of the afternoon chatting while drinking lots of chai. I wasn't needed at Ramana's garden today so it was more of a relaxed afternoon.

I wonder if it's a public holiday today as there were a lot more people about than usual. The bridge was packed with people dressed in beautiful, bright colours, with the occasional motorbike trying to fight its way through the crowd, dealing with traffic jams caused by a cow who decided to lie down in the middle

115

of the bridge.

I would love to bring one of the puppies home with me, but could they survive such a long plane ride? Their home is India. Does it make sense for me to have a dog considering I would like to keep traveling?

I spent the afternoon walking in the mountains and I ran into one of the students, Preethi, after my brief contemplation at the waterfall on my way back down. She and her little sister, Kieran, invited me to their house to meet their mother. Their little brother Raj, who must have been about four years old, came bounding down the hill and gave me a giant hug with a big grin on his face, what a little sweetheart. It's such a different reaction than I would get back home - the kids are so open and friendly here. I rarely see kids playing in the streets where I live back in Canada, it's kind of sad.

We had some chai and sweets and took lots of silly photos together, it's Kieran's birthday tomorrow so they invited me back to join in the celebrations. I think I'll bring them some peanut brittle, as there were some not so subtle hints as to what kind of sweets the kids liked to eat. They live up in the hills, the mother and three kids. They lost their father about a year ago in an accident. I don't know the details, other than it was sudden and unexpected.

I'm thinking of coming back here in September after the monsoon. I'm also thinking of chocolate cake and more chai. Scattered mind, must observe my cravings and diversions. I'm watching the randomness of my thoughts now, my mind is completely scattered today and I'm feeling hyperactive, even a two-hour hike hasn't tired me out, or maybe I just had too much chai earlier today. I must continue to bring more meditation into my daily life if I want to stay sane as my mind is starting to focus too much *on the future again.*

It's a bright sunny day; good times are ahead, even if I did get shit on by a bird this morning. It landed on my cheek and then ran down my t-shirt. People say its good luck, however I think they say that to make you feel better because you have been shit on! Hari-om.

- January 10, 2009 – A drop in the ocean

I am but a drop, I am the ocean. It's pretty amazing, the more I meditate, the more I realize there is so much going on in this crazy mind of mine and it feels like there is an infinite vortex still to be explored. Constantly bombarded by thoughts and stories, it's a wonder my mind doesn't just shut down and take a break. If my body was this busy, I would have died of exhaustion by now! I've learned different types of meditation techniques over the years and sometimes I get visions, like a movie or a kaleidoscope of images that replay in my mind's eye when I sit quietly, sometimes I hear a ringing sound in my ears, sometimes I feel my heartbeat in various parts of my body. Some days are better than others, but then can I really have a bad day meditating? There are days I just don't want to sit still; those are the days to observe what's going on, stepping outside of myself to witness the activity in my mind. When I manage to do this, I notice the agitation usually passes because my mind gets bored easily and is always on the lookout for the next shiny thought.

On the days when I do have more patience and I'm able to go deeper, I'm almost laughing at the chaos that's going on in there. There are constant waves of activity and when I can just watch it all happening, it gives me a little comfort in knowing that this is not really me at the core. Sometimes, even just for a few seconds,

I've experienced a blip of no thoughts, nothingness; Osho calls this 'no-mind.'

Why were we given this ability to constantly think, to obsess over silly details, which we have no control over anyway? Or do we have control? I suppose that's what meditation is all about – learning to control the chaos. Exploring what's going on in here is better than a movie some days; sometimes like a horror movie, or a drama and sometimes it's a comedy, at least it's usually entertaining.

Taming the monkey mind

I had the luxury of spending months in India focusing on my spiritual practice when I had ample time for yoga and meditation - getting to know my inner self and understand the workings of my mind. After the course had ended I had more free time to journal, which was really a way of me dumping my thoughts and observations onto paper. The more I wrote, the more I noticed how random and scattered my thoughts were – I could fluctuate from happy thoughts to sad in a matter of seconds. I could run a particular story in my head about any situation over and over again, making it out to be much worse in my mind compared to reality. It was during meditation where I was able to sit back and observe the stream of thoughts, allowing myself to disconnect with them, even if only for a few moments, which felt like relief.

We all have monkey mind. It's that pesky, mischievous, yet also lovable little voice, or voices, that keep chattering all day long. The monkey hardly ever stops, bouncing around from one thought to the next. Sometimes the monkey is kind and offers supportive thoughts like, 'hey you look pretty good in that shirt,' or 'good job on that presentation today,' and sometimes he can be harsh and say mean things, such as; 'you're not good enough, you're dumb, that girl is prettier than you, you shouldn't have done that.' Most of the time he's just a running commentary reviewing past events and situations that could have gone a different way, or he's wondering about the future – it could be what you're having for dinner tonight, or he could be talking about what you're going to do next year. He hardly ever stops.

While I've been living with my monkey my whole life, we have now come to an understanding that he is not in control – I am. We appreciate each other and I even find him humorous a lot of the time, but he knows his place most of the time. I no longer allow him to direct my life and I don't always have to believe in what he says – especially the negative chatter. I can also take a break from him, even if only for a few moments, to reconnect to my heart during meditation. When you begin to question the monkey and challenge his chatter, you eventually learn that the monkey may not always be right. He can be tamed though, with dedication and persistence and using a variety of tools, one of which is meditation.

What is yoga?

Yoga is a mystical path, an individual journey, lifestyle and path to self-discovery. Yoga encourages me to explore and experience my own truth through direct experiences of higher states of consciousness, of which meditation is the primary way I approach it.

I've spent the past twenty years practicing primarily Hatha and Kundalini yoga. Yoga in the modern world is sometimes confused as mainly being a physical practice or asana only, which is just a small part of it. 'Ha' for the sun, or masculine energy and 'tha' for the moon, or feminine energy, makes up the word 'Hatha.' Hatha, as a tantric path, similar to Kundalini yoga, uses breath work to stimulate and balance the energy in the body through the chakras. It's easy to get confused with all the different traditions, of which often get mistakenly referred to only as class styles of yoga when you read the various descriptions at your local studio or gym.

The meaning of yoga, as translated from Sanskrit, is union. Union of body, mind and spirit; it's the integration of one's thoughts, words, and actions. At the centre is the heart where you can find balance, or harmony within. Thoughts are like a pendulum that swings between happiness and unhappiness and by being present you are able to slow the swing of the pendulum down, or tame the monkey, to a manageable level. For example, if you are in disharmony, if your actions are out of sync with your core beliefs, or if you are thinking about one thing but saying something different, you are not living in alignment or in a state of union. Over time, a persistent and fundamental disconnectedness of thought and action can cause a sense of dis-ease, often manifesting in the body as disease.[1]

According to Patanjali's yoga sutras, yoga is the control of thought waves in your mind. Patanjali was an Indian sage who compiled the sutras (196 aphorisms or truths) around 400 CE as a result of summarizing materials about yoga from previous traditions. "Yoga citta vritti nirodha," is the second sutra and translates to "yoga helps to still, or stop the fluctuations of the mind." These mind fluctuations are repetitive thought patterns that limit you from seeing the truth about yourself, or the world around you.

The truth, as I interpret it, is that we are all one; we all come from the same source of the Divine Creator, yet we so often create barriers that separate us. These can be geographical barriers, race, religion, class, sexual orientation, culture, income, whether we are male or female, etc., there are hundreds of reasons we create to separate ourselves. When you take the time to connect within and with others, you discover that you share the same struggles and fears and insecurities as others, as well as share many of the same successes and ideas that make you happy. When there is too much busyness in the mind, it's easy to get caught up in your thoughts; you spend less time in stillness, less time identifying yourself as spirit.

---

1   Moving into Bliss with Yoga. Chétana Jessica Torrens and Yogi Vishvketu, p 296.

Make space in life for what you wish to manifest. If there is too much busy-ness, the insights and intuitions are buried.
– Chétana Jessica Torrens

How do you meditate?

Meditation is a way to for you to reach a higher state of consciousness. It can bring you back to stillness, back to your natural state of being. For me, meditation is not about sitting still on a yoga mat until my mind clears; rather observing the workings of my mind as I'm sitting still and detaching from the thought process itself. You may still have thoughts, ideas and emotions arising in your mind when you are in a meditative state, however you will be less disturbed by them and they won't distract your focus.

You can also induce more relaxed states and be present through activity. I sometimes experience this in cycling or hiking in nature. Athletes and musicians refer to this as being 'in the zone,' where one is performing an activity where they are fully immersed in a feeling of energized focus and enjoyment in the process of the activity.

> **Reflection:**
> *What does meditation mean to you?*

Why meditate?

What are the results of meditation? There are a variety of ways to practice meditation. The results are unique and will vary by person – it's up to you how you define the results and the difference they are making in your life. People tell me I'm calmer than I used to be, that I have more patience and generally give off a peaceful vibe. I certainly feel more relaxed and centered than I used to be, some of that is from meditation and some I believe

121

comes with age and wisdom. My morning meditation, even if just five or ten minutes, has become an essential part of my daily routine, like brushing my teeth or having my coffee. To help me to feel grounded throughout the day, there are moments where I pause to tune into the present moment by taking a few deep breaths or going for a walk outside, as this provides me with a general feeling of well being.

Practicing daily and having the habit ingrained in me has greatly helped when it comes to dealing with life's larger stresses. Before I was introduced to yoga and meditation I would have likely reacted with anger or aggression, lashing out at the person whom I felt was causing me stress. Nowadays I have much more self-control and am able to step back and observe, and to choose how to act, instead of blindly reacting to situations – my meditation practice is the reason for this. The more you learn about yourself and the nature of your mind through meditation, the more you will become aware of your reactions to people and situations in the moment, allowing you to become more present.

What's getting in your way?

Patanjali writes about obstacles to meditation, which are common distractions that most of us face when we start out and continue to face as experienced meditators. Too often people try meditation for a few days then forget, or life gets in the way and they let their practice go and then feel guilty. When I first started practicing yoga I didn't have a daily meditation practice – my excuse was that I didn't have time to meditate. The truth was that I was not making time for it, nor making it a priority in in my life. Thankfully that excuse is now gone because I've realized the benefits of a daily practice.

Other obstacles, such as; laziness, doubt, lack of enthusiasm, cravings, despair caused by failure to concentrate or sit still, or unrealistic expectations are common. It's important to remember that your practice is always there for you to come back to at any time. Having faith in the process, letting go of judgmental thoughts of yourself and re-committing to yourself to keep trying, is key in dealing with these obstacles when they come up.

Finding your bliss

Samadhi is considered a state of meditative consciousness and has been described as bliss, illumination, or oneness. Being totally aware of the present moment or a single-pointedness of the mind. The state of Samadhi, like the term 'enlightenment', can have many different meanings, depending on whom you ask, as everyone's experience is unique.

While enlightenment or Samadhi may be a goal to some, I perceive it as a state of being that could last a second or even a few minutes, of when I feel completely connected to myself and my surroundings in the present moment. Standing at the top of a mountain, or quietly watching a sunset and feeling at peace, or being in the presence of a loved one and pausing for a moment to acknowledge each other's wonder, or getting caught up in spontaneous and uncontrollable laughter, are all expressions of Samadhi to me. They may be fleeting moments, or they may last longer, but I've found that the more tuned in I am to myself through meditation, the more frequent their occurrences.

It's been said that when you know your mind, you know yourself. This is true because you create your reality through your own mind, you are what you think and you are capable of what you believe. Often the limits you place upon yourself exist only in your mind.

Exercise: Walking Meditation

As I mentioned earlier, meditation isn't solely about sitting still on your yoga mat. You can get yourself into a meditative state, connecting you to the present moment, when you are completely immersed in an activity; one that allows the mind to stop bouncing around from thought to thought. This exercise[2] encourages you to explore meditation as a movement, to really slow down and observe your surroundings. It can be done indoors or outdoors. I particularly enjoy the walking meditation outside, in nature.

You can try this with no particular intent or you may ask a question prior to beginning the exercise, and then let go of any expectation of an answer. Often when I ask a question, the answer is revealed at the end when I notice what I observed during the exercise.

1. Remember to put away your phone and eliminate any other distractions before you begin. You can try this exercise alone, or with a friend and you can discuss your observations afterwards.
2. If you have a question in mind, try to formulate your question as a single sentence, as simply as you can, sticking to one topic or question, rather than a narrative or series of questions bundled together.
3. Repeat your question out loud.
4. No matter where you are, commit to at least ten minutes of walking around in silence. You do not need to have a particular destination, allow yourself to wander.

---

2   Exercise inspired by and used with permission from Barb Pierce of Coaching Horizons.

5. Notice the feeling of your feet on the floor or the ground, walk slowly and deliberately becoming aware of each step at first. This helps to slow the mind down and connect you to your physical body.

6. Observe your surroundings, making no judgments about what you are seeing.

7. Tune into your other senses, what smells, sounds, touch or taste do you notice? It's not necessary that you try to seek out a specific smell or sound, you are scanning your surroundings and taking them in.

8. After a period of time, or whenever you feel ready to stop walking, get out your journal and start jotting down whatever comes to mind first. If you're practicing with a friend, you may journal and/or discuss your observations with your friend. What did you observe during your walk? Did you notice particular patterns in the things you were paying attention to? How did you feel during the exercise? Tuning into your other senses, were there particular sounds or sensations you experienced?

By reviewing your experience with respect to your question, you may find that the answer or some hints to your question were revealed during your walk. For example, we practiced this exercise during a retreat where we had a group of students walk around in the park, one student asked the question about what her greatest personal block was, as she was feeling frustrated with herself and others. During the walk she was particularly drawn to a large rock in the park and could not seem to walk away from it. She noticed the trees and the birds and many other things, yet the rock dominated her experience. She attributed this rock to represent her own stubbornness in life and realized she had to begin to change this and become more free like the birds – this was a revelation for her. Her attitude and energy appeared to have changed for the duration of the retreat. She was more engaged with her surroundings and with the other participants; overall she seemed to be enjoying herself more.

There are no right or wrong answers in how you interpret the meaning of your own experiences for yourself, what's important is that you are willing to explore and allow the answers to be revealed.

Chapter Eleven

- January 12, 2010 – Re-toxing

I missed writing for a couple of days it seems. We had a great weekend Saturday night at Ramana's for pizza and movie (our big night out!). Looking forward to yoga on the beach on Sunday then off to the German bakery to eat everything that is bad for us. I've started teaching some private yoga lessons too, which is great. Today has flown by and I'm looking forward to Kumbh Mela, it's a mass Hindu pilgrimage that happens every four years. The babas will come out from the mountains to offer blessings and to join millions of other people to dip in the Ganga. There's a group of us planning to go to Haridwar later this week and there are many auspicious days for dipping, I've picked 11 times to go for a dip over the course of the celebrations.

I'm feeling a bit distracted still, I couldn't spend a lifetime living in an ashram. I do love it here but I'm wanting to get out and experience a different scene – good thing I have choices. Our little group here is becoming like my second family and it will be sad when we all go our separate ways but such is life.

After detoxing I seem to be re-toxing as I'm eating more junk food than usual, too many pastries at the German bakery and too much chocolate from the general store. Got to find balance as I'm still doing a lot of yoga and meditation. I generally feel better with no alcohol in my system; it's been months now and I don't even miss it. Time for some warm milk from the happy ashram cow, this should do my body good and will make for a good night's sleep. Sweet dreams.

- January 14, 2010 – The release

Viirprit Carney Mudra, or half shoulder stand this morning during Kundalini class seemed to have charged up my sexual energy during meditation. If feels like it has been dispensing throughout my body during the day, either that or I just need to have sex. In this afternoon's class we were dancing and jumping around and I felt like the energy had spread to every cell in my body, which is perhaps why I'm having this creative writing spurt. My pen is moving faster than my mind, or is my mind moving faster than my pen? Either way, my writing is frantic and messy.

I'm not sure what I'm feeling right now because at the end of class I was happily smiling from ear-to-ear and everything felt right in the world, then at dinner I felt like I didn't want to finish my food and I had to get out of there quickly, I was so irritated. How convenient, I have been shuffling through the iPod to find the right song and Marvin Gaye has arrived with Sexual Healing. There is definitely a strong energy moving in my body.

I love this new state of being, ever since the yoga teacher training 500-hour course, I feel more in tune with myself, especially on the subtle body level, I'm starting to get chills over my whole body just writing about it. I need to just feel this as it moves through me and around me. It's really bizarre, my chest is warm and my arms are tingling and my fingertips are cold. The more

I inhale and focus on my fingers, the more they tingle. I don't think its caffeine, as I haven't had chai since this morning. The tingling and sensations are a mild form of what I experienced a few weeks ago, the night I missed the kirtan and had a meltdown, maybe it's time to finally write about that. I've been avoiding it and before I was thinking of it as indescribable. When I look back at the timing of that craziness, the previous week was focused mostly on Kundalini classes, so maybe that's why things got so stirred up.

That night after dinner, when people were getting ready for kirtan, I started to feel like I was having flu-like symptoms, with a really strange feeling in the pit of my stomach, hot and cold flashes and a bit of nausea – I was wondering if I had eaten something that wasn't agreeing with me. I talked to Vishva to let him know I wasn't feeling so great and may not make it to kirtan, then went back to my room and went to bed. I wrapped up in blankets but nothing could stop the shivering; my body was so cold and I felt like I was going to throw up. I decided to jump in the shower hoping really hot water would warm me up, but that didn't work so I got out of the shower still freezing and climbed back into bed and just curled up into a ball. I closed my eyes and then a vision came - it was a night many years ago from when I was living in Vancouver and I was having sex with Adam, it was towards the end of our relationship. I really wasn't into it at the time and I asked him to stop, but he didn't, so I asked him again and still he didn't stop so I just laid there and waited for it to be over, silently crying to myself. I didn't know if he heard me.

As this vision was coming I needed to put my hands between legs over my crotch. An intense pain started to well up from deep inside me, and all I could think of was just to keep my hands *there tightly protecting that part of my body. Then suddenly this wave of emotion came over me and I started shaking and I was thinking this is one hell of a flu - what is going on?*

The shaking got more intense and it felt like something was starting to take over my body, like an exorcism, as I was crying and shaking uncontrollably for what seemed to be a lifetime, but it went on for about 45 minutes. Eventually I started to catch my breath and I laid there on my bed completely still, wrapped up in my blankets, just trying to figure out what had just happened. Maybe this was some kind of release? I managed to get myself back into the bathroom, although my legs were weak, and I could barely carry my own weight, I blew my nose and got a glass of water and I just sat there on my bed staring at the wall and feeling in shock, not understanding what had just happened.

Next, my instinct had me lying on the floor on my yoga mat and I placed my metal tea cup under my right hip where I've had that pain in my piriformis muscle. I just laid there until I could fully feel my body again. It took about an hour for the numbness to go away. I finally mustered up the energy and got back into bed. Barb came back from kirtan and I tried to put into words what I had just experienced. She was really supportive and just listened to my experience. I'm getting tired just writing about it and my pen is slowing down on the page. It feels ok to write about it though. Maybe now I can finally put it behind me. Time for sleep.

- January 16, 2010 – Finding balance

I'm cutting back on chocolate and sweet treats from the German Bakery for a while; it's time to get back in balance. I think I went too far with the detoxing, which is probably why I've gone overboard on eating so many sweets lately. I feel a little more in control and less frantic over having chocolate after every meal.

Love cannot be created, cultivated, contrived, or thought to be achieved; it's something that happens, sometimes you feel it creeping up and sometimes it hits you like a smack in the face. I read this somewhere and now I can't remember where, it must be in one of the five books I'm reading! Not sure I want a smack in the face but I feel I can create and cultivate love – is this not what I've been doing these past few months? Cultivating it for myself? Starting first with what I put into my body in the form of food for nourishment.

The dogs are barking outside, I had better go check on them; normally they're not this frantic.

The path to healing

That night I experienced the flu-like symptoms, along with the 45 minutes of uncontrollable shaking and crying was the final straw of me physically releasing a painful past experience that I had suppressed. It was time for me to let go of old stories, which I believe also led to the spontaneous healing of the persistent pain in my right hip. My body was storing painful emotions, which were built up during my relationship with Adam and had manifested into a physical pain. The release wasn't just about that night when we were having sex and he didn't stop; my body was releasing the pain from emotional abuse. I had become a shell of my former self in that relationship. I had believed all of the awful things that I was being told about myself that were mixed in with the 'I love you's'; the negative words that led to a lot of self-doubt. It took me two days to fully feel back to normal after that night, I was exhausted.

I realize now that my meditation and yoga practice helped to clear the way for the healing to occur. Practicing yoga daily allowed me to explore the emotions and feelings I was experiencing in my body. Sitting still in meditation was a challenge for me at times because painful memories would surface, causing me to face the emotional pain again. The mind consists of three levels; conscious, subconscious and unconscious. If you're like many people you may have noticed that your mind is very busy but surprisingly it can only do one thing at a time. It processes information so quickly that it might seem like it's capable of multitasking. The subconscious mind is there to take the overflow, especially when the conscious mind can't make a decision or is unable to process a situation as it is happening. Think of all your unfinished business or actions collecting in your subconscious!

How do you clear your unconscious mind?

Meditation opens the door to the unconscious mind to bring the unfinished business back to the surface so it can be dealt with or released. The ego can make excuses and will try to convince you to leave that 'stuff' alone. Having a regular meditation practice, even for a few minutes a day, helps to settle the conscious mind and allows the subconscious and unconscious mind to reveal the stuff (stories or karmic patterns) to be released, which ultimately brings more lightness to your being.

Releasing emotional baggage

I believe you can store emotions from your experiences anywhere in your body, including your organs. Emotional storage gets built up over time from smaller experiences, or they can get trapped due to a major traumatic event. If you don't have a way to process your emotions, they can often turn into physical pain or disease.

Reflection:

What kind of physical symptoms do you experience in your body when you feel stressed?

Shaking the trauma off

In his book Healing Trauma, Peter Levine proposes that trauma can have an effect on the body in a variety of ways, many of which may not show up for years after the initial trauma has occurred. Defining trauma is challenging – ultimately you become traumatized when your ability to respond to a *perceived* threat is in some way overwhelmed. There are obvious traumas, such as; war, childhood sexual abuse, or being a victim of a violent attack, loss of a loved one, etc., and not so obvious, such as; minor car accident, illness, being left alone (especially as a baby or young child), being called names or being the victim of bullying. Levine explains that trauma is about a loss of connection to yourself, your body, your family, to others, and to the world around you. These changes can happen subtly and over time and often you adapt to them without noticing them.[1]

Levine observed the behaviour of animals in the wild, which are routinely threatened by their prey, and noticed they are rarely traumatized. Animals seem to have a built-in ability to literally shake off the effects of life-threatening encounters, whereas we humans do not.[2] Or in my case, I did shake it off years after the original event happened. If you are looking to heal a past trauma it's important that you seek assistance from mental health and medical professionals where appropriate, so you are not dealing with it alone. I kept the secret of my unhealthy relationship hidden from friends and family for a long time. The rest of this chapter will focus on explaining more about the energetic body and understanding how to tune in and interpret the en-

---

1   Healing Trauma, Peter Levine, page 9.

2   Healing Trauma, Peter Levine, page 25.

ergy and signals from your body, it is not intended to be your sole resource for healing major trauma.

Be good to your body

Whether you are on a yogic path or not, it's necessary to pay attention to the state of your physical body and what you are offering it in the form of food, water, exercise and rest. Having a healthy body as a foundation supports you in going deeper into exploring additional layers of yourself through meditation.

Early in 2010 when I was living in India for six months I had not had any alcohol and the ashram vegetarian diet for my main meals was generally healthy. However I noticed I was writing a lot about the chai I was drinking and sweet treats I was eating daily. I felt that my morning was not complete if I didn't have chai. I was wondering if I had swapped out one addiction for another – alcohol for caffeine and sugar. I went on a three-day juice fast and also tried shankprakshalana – a salt-water cleansing technique where I drank up to 4-litres of saltwater and performed a series of yoga asanas until my stool was clear. It's a technique you should not try on your own the first time!

During these periods of detox I was hyper-aware of my food cravings, especially because I was on a very restricted diet of rice and lentils for a week after shankprakshalana. I began to notice how my emotions were connected to my food cravings; for example, I would feel anxious and sometimes angry that I could not have chocolate. Some of the emotions were related to the physical detox, getting my body used to not relying on sugar. Most of the emotions were related to my feeling of a lack of control over what I could and could not eat – that was where the anger came in. Once I understood more about the roots of my cravings I realized I had the power to choose differently and not give into them. Nowadays I rarely have caffeine; however, I am still working on the chocolate cravings.

Practice tuning into your body wisdom

Your body is full of wisdom and is constantly sending you messages through your feelings and emotions. You have the innate ability to tune in to receive the messages, when you take the time to do it. Building up your emotional awareness is done by listening to your body and using this information in everyday life. By doing this, you can learn to be more present and more aware of your current situation, which allows you to respond appropriately.

For example, a few years ago I went for a job interview. The position sounded perfect on paper and I was happy that I was called in for an interview after applying. When I first arrived at the office, everything seemed great; people were friendly, the hiring manager was happy and welcoming, and then the interview started. A few minutes in, I noticed that my chest was feeling constricted, so I adjusted my body position to sit up straighter and took a few deep breaths, thinking it might have been nerves. I answered all the questions that were asked but noticed there was little friendly dialogue in between questions; it was more like me getting grilled to see how fast I could respond. I was still feeling slightly constricted in my chest, my belly felt heavy and based on the questions that were being asked, I was getting the sense that the role that was originally described may not be the reality of the day-to-day job; something didn't feel right.

Then it came my turn to ask questions, so I asked a few clarifying questions to test out what my body was telling me. I asked how they liked to have fun and how they celebrated successes together because I was getting the impression it was all work and no play. The interviewer's body language completely changed, there was less eye contact and her words didn't match her posture. She was saying all the right things, but her body language was not open, confident, nor at ease. Either she had already decided I was not the right candidate for the job or else perhaps she was not being 100% forthcoming about the reality of the work culture and the demands of the job. We wrapped up the interview and I left the office with an incredible headache – a clear sign to me to not go back for a second interview.

Without this awareness, many years ago I would have ignored these sig-nals from my body and would have gone back for a second interview. I might have even taken the job, only to find out later that it really wasn't the best fit for me. Thankfully my intuition and the messages from my body, led me elsewhere.

Repeating the past

You are not your past. I am not my past. I am no longer the person shrouded in self-doubt and feeling shame for staying in a relationship that was not good for me. You have the ability to start anew each day, or in any giv-en moment. You often attract situations and people into your life to bring awareness to the surface of that which you need to address or heal. If you are disconnected from your emotions and your body, you tend to repeat these patterns, often until you reach a breaking point.

Use your daily experiences as a mirror, noticing what surfaces in your mind and body as you go about your day and interact with people. While it may not be appropriate to transform and clear a situation the moment it presents itself, I hope that by now you are realizing the importance of taking time to yourself each day to reflect, whether it's sitting quietly, or journaling or doing some other activity that allows you to connect to yourself, to your inner wisdom, to the Divine.

Exercise: Ask your body a question

You can seek guidance by asking a question of your body (your inner guide or intuition) on your own. I've done this exercise many times and some days the signals just aren't there or I'm too distracted. Most days the answers arrive with ease. It's important to keep trying and don't beat yourself up if your inner wisdom is not cooperating on a given day. See if you can have fun and experiment with it.

1. Find a time and space where it will be quiet when you will have no interruptions.
2. Either sitting or lying down, take a few relaxing breaths.
3. Ask your body for support in answering your question.
4. Ask your question. Try to keep the question short and simple, for example 'What do I need to know right now regarding looking for another job?' or 'What do I need to learn about my relationship with my brother?'
5. Close your eyes and focus on your breathing, taking slow, deep breaths. Be patient and wait for the answers to be revealed.

The answer may come in the form of a word, a thought or a symbol that comes to mind. You may experience a physical sensation in a certain part of your body. If you experience a physical sensation, allow yourself to focus in on that area. Imagine you are breathing into that area, noticing if the sensation passes or gets stronger. When you continue to ask questions, putting yourself into a state of inquiry, it opens you up to finding meaning in your situation, often leading to a solution, instead of focusing on the problem itself. Only you can assign meaning to the messages you are receiving.

Chapter Twelve Take Action

- January 17, 2010 – Monster

It's been a busy time lately, even though the course is done and I'm supposed to be taking it easy. I've managed to fill my days teaching yoga, volunteering, and taking harmonium, drumming and singing lessons.

On a sad note, the chaos of the dogs barking yesterday was likely because Jackie, or aka Monster (the biggest dog who was my favourite) was really sick and died sometime in the night. She was being really shy when I last saw her and it felt like she was avoiding me, but now I realize she probably wanted to be on her own to die. I've read that animals do that when they know their time has come. I'm glad I got to pet her and spend some quality time with her, even if I didn't know then it was her last night. I saw her little lifeless body earlier, just lying there and the smallest puppy, Julie was lying beside her. The three of them came over to see me for their kisses and cuddles and they were crying, it was so sad but for some reason I didn't cry and I still haven't. I'm wondering if it's coming when I least expect it. I feel mellow and want to keep to myself for the rest of the night. The construction site manager says he will give her a nice burial, or least that's what I understood from my limited Hindi. Yet anoth-

er one has succumbed to rabies.

When I returned from the market this afternoon, Swami Am-lanand was waiting for me in the ashram library. I have no idea how long he was waiting, nor was I expecting him, but he just showed up from Haridwar, maybe from Vishva's request, to offer advice about how to establish Helping Hands for India as a charity. We've come a long way since I offered to write the marketing brochure a few weeks ago. I've been working on the website and it's coming along nicely. I remember our last chat as I had all these big ideas and he told me to keep it simple, take it one day at a time – good advice for me, as I like to juggle lots of projects. You can't always plan here, it's India, there's a certain amount of going with the flow needed, or hari-om as they say.

- January 23, 2010 – Good times

After a few days of being alone and finally crying over the loss of Monster, the last three days have been all about celebrating, Ganga-dipping, dancing and eating amazing food. We all piled into the tuk tuk to go to Haridwar and we braved the rushing and freezing waters at the Har Ki Puri ghat to ask for blessings of Mother Ganga and to cleanse us of stuff we no longer need.

Kumbh Mela is in full swing and there are millions of people about. The crowds can be a little overwhelming but it's a fun atmosphere. The six of us managed to stick together. On the way back our tuk tuk driver had a fondness for really loud Bollywood music and it was blaring for most of the one-hour journey. We stopped about half way and got out at the side of the road for a spontaneous dance party. Later we pulled into the fancy Vasund-hara Palace restaurant and continued to dance in the parking lot, much to the dismay of the doorman and the delight of onlookers, it was hilarious.

I've started reading Autobiography of a Yogi by Paramhansa Yogananda and it's now 8:55 pm so I don't think I'll get very far tonight since it's almost my bedtime. It's got me hooked though and I'm excited to read more tomorrow. He talks about his memories as an infant and some of the incredible insights he's seen since birth. How amazing would it be to remember all of that?

Today's class was focusing on Ajna chakra, and we've been working our way up through the chakras this week. I will seek more direction from my dreams. So many ideas and visions and plans, where does one start? I have faith and I trust the universe will show me the way. In the meantime, I'm going to keep enjoying the festivities of Kumbh Mela and will keep working on the Helping Hands for India website!

Balancing effort and allowing

Balancing action versus allowing things to happen is something I've found challenging, as I'm an action-oriented person. I don't like sitting around waiting for things to happen. However, as much as I know I can get things done myself, some of my greater accomplishments have been when I've let go and not been caught up in action. Rather I've been in a state of openness and receptivity, allowing the help from outside sources and synchronicity to provide the very assistance I need.

Writing this book is a perfect example. While I've been writing in my journal for years and have made passing comments about wanting to write a book, I had not pursued it seriously until 2016. Had I attempted this fifteen years ago I would not have had the wisdom and experience to offer that I do today. When the idea to write the book came back again early in 2016, suddenly an offer to attend a free writer's workshop came my way – this was enough to get me motivated and to start taking the idea seriously. Some of my recent life experiences have served as inspiration to tie the content together. When I started sharing with people that I was writing a book, I was then introduced to people who would help me along the way. I've learned a lot about publishing, marketing, and editing as a result.

You're part of a bigger plan

Taking time to slow down and leaving space for the *allowing* to happen opens up the opportunity for outside sources to come to your assistance. These outside sources can be thought of as the Divine, the Universe, or God, or whatever you identify with. I recognize this help as it comes in the form of synchronicity. I know and trust now that I do not control everything. I'm participating in the co-creation of part of a bigger plan for my life. There is some relief for me in knowing this as it reassures me that I don't have to have all the answers right now.

When I feel like I'm working too hard and pushing up against too many roadblocks on a particular project then I know it's time to take a step back, to stop working so hard trying to force things my way. It's at these moments that I receive the divine guidance that I need, whether it's a vision that comes to me in meditation that tells me what my next step should be, or someone shows up in my life to offer guidance or I just happen to be in the right place at the right time to gain a new perspective about my situation. Help can arrive in many forms, whether it's from another person, an animal, in nature, a seemingly random phone call from an old friend, you name it, every moment there is a chance to receive insight. The best way for me to notice synchronous events is to slow down and to notice what is going on around me in the present moment.

Taking small steps

After a few months of living the ashram life in India and dealing with the pendulum of my emotions and cravings and healing old pain I felt like I was settling into a nice rhythm of life. I was becoming more focused on what I could do to give back.

We were looking into getting the charity legally registered in Canada so that we could connect interested sponsors (mostly yoga teachers) with students who lived near the ashram, which would give the program more structure. Vishva had already been supporting some of the local children, providing financial support for school uniforms and books. The more we started talking about the sponsorship program, the more yoga teachers wanted to get involved. In the span of a year we had fifteen students sponsored to go to school. It all started with my teacher's vision to help children. We didn't know at that time how our organization would continue to grow in the years to come.

While there is a certain element of action and allowing when you want to bring a dream to life, nothing will happen if you don't take that first step. Some people are visionaries, some are more detail and task-oriented, which is why it's important to surround yourself with people who will encourage and support you. Look for people who can work together with you, to help you turn your dreams into reality. Sometimes all you need to do is reach out and ask for help. Try not to take rejection personally; if your request for help isn't answered the first time you ask, seek other resources.

Reflection:

I want you to fast-forward to your last day on earth and imagine looking back over what you are most proud of. Have you achieved this yet? If not, what is the next smallest step you can take to get you closer to your goal?

Coming back to the questions I posed in the beginning of this book: How big are your dreams? What will it cost you not to pursue them? If there were no limits and no judgments, what would you be doing? What's stopping you from taking the first smallest step? Having persistence, determination and a belief that you can accomplish whatever you set your mind to, is a powerful combination that will get you so much closer to a state of *living* a life you love, not just imagining it.

 *The mind is everything. What you think you become. - Buddha*

Mind practices can enhance your motivation, increase confidence and prime your brain for success. Combining the visualization with feeling adds more power to your vision. Through all the challenges you will face in life, when you are able to exert a great deal of control over the way you talk to yourself, you will reduce or evict the negative voices living in your head that tell you that you can't do something.

A new perspective on failure

Revisiting themes from earlier in the book, remember to let go of fear and judgment when it comes to pursuing your dreams. Fear of failure or of not achieving something is what commonly stops many people from taking the first step. Failure exists if you let it and you are *not* defined by mistakes. What if failure could be considered an opportunity to learn and a chance to change course on your path? Since there are many different ways to reach the end goal, your cue as to when you may be off course is when you are not feeling at ease with yourself. When this happens, get still and ask yourself what is the next smallest step you can take, and take that next step.

Looking back through my past, I could easily judge myself by thinking that I stayed in an emotionally abusive relationship for too long, or that I uprooted myself too many times by moving from city to city. However I don't see my experiences as mistakes; I see them as life experiences that have provided me the opportunity to learn and to have compassion for myself now. I'm

143

LIFE REBOOT

much more aware now when I'm not feeling at ease with myself, which gives me the power to choose differently moving forward.

Roadblocks to moving forward

There are common roadblocks that many people face when it comes to taking action and moving forward on your path. Do you have regrets? Do you find yourself lamenting over the past, wishing you had acted or said something differently in a particular situation? Or even wishing you had chosen a different path in life? I've often replayed situations in my mind hundreds of times over, where I wished I had said something different, wished I had behaved differently towards someone. The continuous replay in my mind doesn't serve me. Instead I've learned to make amends and apologize when I can if I've made a mistake. If I don't have the opportunity to offer an apology then I need to forgive myself and move on instead of focusing on the past situation that I cannot change anyway.

If you are the king or queen of 'should have' or 'could have', instead of focusing on the past, ask yourself how you will be the next time a similar situation comes up so that you can do better in the future. When you are frequently living in the past wondering what you could have or should have done, it's self-defeating and a drain on your energy. It takes time away from moving you forward towards what you really want to accomplish. You may have to drop the behaviour hundreds of times before it goes away. Once you are aware of this habit and you catch yourself dwelling on past, negative experiences, change your thoughts to something positive and don't judge yourself for having this habit. Over time you will train your mind to be present and to have a forward focus.

Another common roadblock is lack of motivation. There are various reasons for lack of motivation, sometimes people don't start a project because it may seem overwhelming and too big to accomplish and they're not sure where to start. I suggest you start from where you are, with the resources that

144

you currently have. Once you have a vision of where you want to go, how you want to be, or what you want to accomplish, and start to break it down into achievable tasks and you start taking action – even a really small action step – you are getting that much closer to your goals.

Notice when you're going off track

Notice when the action steps you are taking may be out of alignment with your intention, meaning when you feel like you are going through the motions and you are no longer enjoying pursuing your goal. It's important to choose joyful tasks and to have fun with what you are doing. This is not to say that there won't be challenges and that you should avoid anything unpleasant, rather to notice when the majority of what you are doing is causing you frustration or doesn't feel good. It may be time to step back and re-evaluate why you are pursuing this particular goal or set of tasks.

Exercise: Hold Yourself Accountable

If you have been following along with the exercises in this book, you have been taking lots of action steps to get to know yourself and your inner world, which is primarily what drives your outer world experience. Ultimately you are responsible for holding yourself accountable. You have the power to create the circumstances in your world for a joyful and abundant life. Now is the time to check in, to acknowledge how far you've come and to evaluate if there is a particular area that needs more attention.

1. Have you done all of the exercises in the book so far?
2. Have you done some of the exercises but have skipped a few?
3. If you have skipped some or all of the exercises in this book, ask yourself why. Be honest with yourself.

By completing the above exercise, you have already taken your next smallest action step. As you are taking more action steps it's important to recognize and celebrate your accomplishments on your journey. Acknowledge what is going well and celebrate milestones by treating yourself somehow. Life is a journey, not a destination, right?

Chapter Thirteen Conclusion

- July 4, 2011 – True love

According to Osho, first be happy, be joyful, be celebrating and then you will find some other soul celebrating and there will be a meeting of two dancing souls and a great dance will arise out of it and when you are ready to love somebody a beautiful relationship will arise. Love yourself, forgive yourself over and over, then you will flower, only then there is a relationship which has grace, which has beauty, which has benediction in it. If you can find such a relationship, your relationship will grow into prayer, your love will become an ecstasy, a true love and you will know what the Divine is.

I love Osho, that's what I will bring into my life. I will imagine that it's already here. I've met many wonderful men on my travels but not much has materialized into anything long term – that's a topic for a whole other book, and I certainly haven't experienced anything like Osho has described, but that doesn't mean it's not possible.

Time to stop writing and get back to work, I have a few hours to put in this afternoon then I'm off to the clinic to teach yoga. I'm working from my balcony on a gorgeous hot day, how can it get better than this?

- October 31, 2011 – Goodbye Bali, for now

Happy 90th birthday Grandma! I'm now at Denpasar airport, my noodles have arrived and I'm sitting here with mixed feelings. I'm feeling a little drained, a result of going to bed the last three nights at 4 am, and because it's been an emotional day saying goodbye to everyone at Bumi Sehat Clinic, Eka and the family and my friends. It's amazing how one can fit into a community in such a short time. It's been a blast, it's been heart opening and while I'm sad I'm also sitting with a feeling of gratitude and happiness.

Every ending is a new beginning as they say. I'm off to a totally different scene and I'll get to catch up with friends and family in Ireland, Scotland and England. The temperature change is going to be a shock; I'm showing up in flip-flops, as I don't have any other shoes. I'll also need to get a winter jacket as I could be going on a European tour. All of this is to be sorted when I get to London. If I get this next job I could end up being the manager of a rock band. How on earth did this happen? Let the fun continue…

Thriving in the present

When I took the time to notice I realized I had created and was living a life I had dreamt of when I first left for India back in 2008. My travels through Asia continued, I spent a few months in Laos and a few more in Thailand. I had explored Malaysia and Borneo, Fiji, and other parts of Indonesia before landing in Bali for six months to volunteer teaching yoga at Bumi Sehat, the birthing clinic.

148

I was working at a company that allowed me the luxury and freedom to earn a living from wherever I chose to live. When I left Bali I was heading to London, England to meet with the public relations manager of a major rock band as I had the opportunity to become their tour manager, along with a dear friend of mine. This opportunity eventually fell through, and probably for the best as I can only imagine life on the road with a rock band would have been chaotic and would have involved lots of drugs and booze.

I had traveled quite a lot in my twenties but it was different from the years of travel I experienced in my thirties. I felt like less of a tourist, spending months in a particular location allowed me to experience more of the culture and I got to know the local people more than if I was passing through for a week.

While my scenery was frequently changing, what had changed the most was me. I had made peace with the past regarding my intimate relationships. I had also let go of a lot of unnecessary anger and self-indulgent behaviour that wasn't serving me, such as drinking and smoking pot daily. I was feeling and becoming more whole and didn't need external fixes to make me feel better. My journey to my inner self, getting to know the real me through yoga and meditation, has changed my life for the better as I've learned how to manage my emotions in a positive way and to embrace the flow of life's events instead of unnecessary reactions and over-analyzing situations. While I do still make mistakes, I'm more forgiving of myself and others and I don't allow negative emotions to linger.

- December 17, 2016 – My purpose

The purpose of my life is to love, to give and receive love, to be love. To love and accept myself unconditionally. To love and accept others exactly as they are. To live in a happy and healthy environment and to make the most of what I have. My purpose is to give back, to take care of myself physically and emotionally so that I am better able to serve others. My purpose is to live my best life; to laugh often and to find joy in everything. My purpose is to connect with the Divine and to appreciate every moment. Infinite love is already here. It's within me and always has been. Looking back I see that I had forgotten it and I was seeking it everywhere but from within. Someone said to me recently 'you have no idea how beautiful you are.' Sometimes certain people show up to remind you what you have forgotten. I have also forgiven myself, and others, for any mistreatment in my life. I have healed the wounds from my past. I feel liberated. Everything makes sense now.

The more I tend to feeling good and recognizing the God within me and around me, the more my light shines and the better off everyone is who comes into contact with me. When I'm seeking that love outside of myself, whether through another person, through alcohol or food, or any other distraction, my light dulls and I lose my inner connection to God and to the beauty of everything that is.

As Osho said, love yourself, forgive yourself over and over, then you will flower.

When I can maintain the feeling of self-love and I come across another soul who also maintains it - and we can both recognize when we get off track and can support each other to return home - that is Divine love in union with another. Divine love in union with another is just around the corner for me and I'm excited to see it unfold.

Recreating yourself in every moment

Reflecting upon where I am at today, life is both cyclical and open ended. Here I am back in Vancouver and everything has come full circle. This is where I ended my relationship with Adam almost ten years ago. I left this city to embark on years of travel and adventure and I've come back home, back home to myself. I'm not sure what the future holds but I know it will be one filled with love and joy because I have a renewed relationship with myself.

It really is all about the journey, and not the destination. The beauty of life is that you are always creating; you always have a chance to start anew and to recreate yourself with every moment. To experience lasting change in your life is about taking small steps and sometimes big leaps, recommitting to yourself and the process of learning and self-discovery. It's about being forgiving when mistakes are made, allowing you to continuously learn how to be different, to respond differently and to become a better person while learning from your experiences. It's about choosing new perspectives, adopting new healthy beliefs and leaving behind old stories, not allowing them to define you for the rest of your life.

 To finish the moment, to find the journey's end in every step of the road, to live the greatest number of good hours, is wisdom.
– Ralph Waldo Emerson

Helping Hands, Caring Hearts

I'm passionate about using education to change the world. You have probably heard of the proverb "Give a man a fish and you feed him for a day; teach a man to fish and you feed him for a lifetime." In 2009 in India, when I offered to write a brochure for Vishva for the local kids he was sponsoring, I had no idea at the time that this would be the start of a much bigger initiative that has grown over the years into an international charity – Helping Hands for India. It's an accomplishment that I'm really proud of.

Early in 2010, when I was living in India for six months after my second yoga teacher training, I had more time to dedicate to getting Helping Hands for India off the ground. I had spent some time writing content and building the Helping Hands for India website and it was nearing completion. Vishva was also talking about building a school in the future and I wanted to be a part of this project. I had the opportunity to travel in Northern India, visiting local schools and orphanages which was helping me to learn more about the education system and the problems that we could help address with our school.

One afternoon I went to visit a school and ashram with Vishva – this particular visit left an impression on me. Maharishi Dayanand Vidyalya and Viklan is in a rural area a few hours drive from Rishikesh and there are 160 children attending, some who have physical disabilities from polio. It was heartbreaking to see some of the little ones crawling around on their hands and knees without full use of their legs. We were given a tour and stopped to see their fully functioning cowshed, which they were immensely proud of, and stopped by a few of the classrooms to meet some of the children.

What struck me was the level of respect the young students had for visitors and teachers. The entire class was the standing at the same time, waiting for direction from the principal with big smiles and Namaste. I felt humbled by the visit and was emotional afterwards, realizing how many things are taken for granted, especially back home where we typically are well provided for both medically and financially. I felt like any troubles I was facing at that time paled in comparison to a child who is not able to walk simply because they don't have access to a vaccine for a preventable disease.

Why give back?

Seva, or selfless service, is defined as a service that is performed without any expectation of result or reward. These services are performed to benefit other human beings or society in general. There are thousands of ways in which you can be of service to others in big or small ways. Holding a door for someone, smiling at your neighbours, picking up garbage that has been thrown into the street, meditation for peace, are just some examples of how you can make a difference and they don't cost anything.

Small acts of kindness have a ripple effect on others and it's often paid forward. You never know how much you will impact others when you show you care. The act and spirit of giving connects you to your community, both near and far. If you're feeling alone, when you reach out to someone to offer your help, you quickly realize you're not alone and that you are not the only person who is struggling in this world.

On my last day in India in the spring of 2010 I went into a local shop to look at crystals. The shop owner informed me he was a palm reader and offered to read my fortune. "You need to offer service to others in order to invite more joy and good things into your life," was what he said. Those were wise words and practical advice that I've been following for many years now. As I sometimes tend to get wrapped up in my thoughts and my own world, I've found one of the best ways to feel appreciation for others is to give back and volunteer my time with people and for causes that I'm passionate about.

 Never doubt that a small group of thoughtful committed citizens can change the world; indeed, it's the only thing that ever has. – Margaret Mead

The formation of Helping Hands for India is living proof of the truth behind Margaret Mead's words. When I left India in 2010 I had no idea when I would return, but I knew that I would go back. It was over the course of the next three years that I traveled to many different countries finding ways to volunteer through teaching yoga supporting local, community projects.

I returned to India once a year as the school transformed from an idea into reality, going from design to construction during 2012 and 2013. The school officially opened its doors and welcomed about two hundred children on July 1, 2014. We have been fortunate to have the support of so many people along the way. Hundreds of people have played a part in making this project come to life by offering their time, money, expertise and hard labour.

The more you give, the more you do receive. This is not to say that you give so that you can receive but when you give your time, money, energy, expertise, love or compassion, or something else to another, without an expectation of receiving anything in return, both of you are better off. We live in an abundant universe and the act of giving allows the energy to flow outwards to someone while also creating space for more energy to flow back to you in the form of receiving.

154

Start small and be open to the flow of giving and receiving. You have no control over how or when the energy is returned and if you keep making space for it, by giving without expectation, you will invite more positive things into your life by the very fact that you are going with the natural flow of energy, rather than resisting it. When you can take delight in another's success, without thinking 'what about me,' this is a sign you are on the right track.

Imagine if everyone had the same opportunities in life. While we're not all born into the same circumstances, we do have the power to change our circumstances. We all have the ability to change ourselves for the better and to offer help to others to make life a little easier for all. Imagine what's possible if we all gave just a little bit. I believe it's the small things that add up to make a big difference.

As of 2017 Helping Hands is expanding again. We have raised funds to build two new classrooms, allowing us to support children up to eighth grade. The people in the village are eagerly awaiting us to build a high school. You can learn more about our organization and follow our progress at http://helpinghandsforindia.org/.

Recommended Reading

Autobiography of a Yogi, Paramhansa Yogananda.

Healing Trauma: A Pioneering Program for Restoring the Wisdom of Your Body, Peter A. Levine, Ph.D.

Kundalini Tantra, Swami Satyananda Saraswati.

Spiritual Partnership: The Journey to Authentic Power, Gary Zukav.

The Tao of Writing: Imagine. Create. Flow, Ralph L. Wahlstrom.

The Wisdom of Yoga: A Seeker's Guide to Extraordinary Living, Stephen Cope.

What God Said: The 25 Core Messages of Conversations With God That Will Change Your Life and The World, Neale Donald Walsch.